THE DESIGN OF INSIGHT

THE DESIGN OF INSIGHT

How to Solve Any Business Problem

M I H N E A   C .   M O L D O V E A N U

A N D   O L I V I E R   L E C L E R C

stanford briefs
An Imprint of Stanford University Press
Stanford, California

Stanford University Press
Stanford, California

Printed in the United States of America

Library of Congress Cataloging-in-Publication Data

Moldoveanu, Mihnea C., author.
The design of insight : how to solve any business problem /
Mihnea C. Moldoveanu and Olivier Leclerc.
pages cm
Includes bibliographical references.
ISBN 978-0-8047-9409-1 (pbk. :   )
1. Problem solving. 2. Insight. 3. Industrial management. I. Leclerc,
Olivier, (Business consultant), author. II. Title.
HD30.29.M58 2015
658.4'03—dc23
2015004647

ISBN 978-0-8047-9579-1 (electronic)

Typeset by Bruce Lundquist in 10/13 Adobe Garamond

CONTENTS

PREFACE

This is not merely a book but a platform for defining, structuring, and solving business problems. Business problems are not like math problems, economics problems, or engineering problems: they are more like quandaries, issues, predicaments, and situations that must be defined before they are solved. To be defined, they must be articulated, and the basic disciplines of business and management to date have tried to sweep the difficulty of defining problems under the rugs of their own language systems. What we do here is lay bare this black box of business problem definition and break it down so that it can be mastered and practiced in any business domain. To do so, we introduce a set of powerful, universal modeling languages that will allow you to represent any issue, predicament, or difficulty in any one of five problem-solving languages: languages that will let you build models of the predicament that will give you a well defined problem to solve. We call these languages *flexons* (flexible objects for the generation of novel solutions).

Model-based problem solving—the discipline our platform teaches and gives you practice with—is useful not only because it allows you to generate precise, deep, and accurate problem statements in any domain of business practice, but also because it allows you to design your problem-solving process for insight.

Having five modeling languages is more than five times more valuable than having one, because business problems are unlikely to yield to insights generated from any one language alone and far more likely to yield to an adaptive tool kit of languages. We will show you both why and how.

Like any other discipline, practice is paramount, so our platform is relentlessly practice oriented. Each modeling tool kit comes with a set of training examples that are drawn from actual business scenarios and predicaments and are either current or have occurred very recently. By the end of the training sequence, you will have seen, defined, and solved problems ranging from smart phone design to currency trading, from executive team mismanagement to vertical integration in the auto industry, and from pharmaceuticals research and development process improvement to private equity deal flow optimization.

We offer our deep and sincere thanks to Margo Beth Fleming, our editor, who insightfully guided our efforts throughout; Raluca Cojocariu for her tireless editorial assistance and support; Alex Yeo who provided helpful comments and suggestions on several drafts of the book; and Graham Huber, who helped define and design a graphical language that makes flexons more intuitive and vivid than any of us could have made them.

THE DESIGN OF INSIGHT

1 WHAT IS THIS ALL ABOUT?

Innovative solutions to complex business problems are like works of art: they elicit emotions similar to the ones we feel in front of great paintings or photographs. They transform our views of the world by showing it to us from different perspectives. When Yann Arthus-Bertrand shows us a photograph of the earth from the sky, it not only expands our horizons in the literal sense but reveals unsuspected patterns in the landscapes we thought we knew well.

A new theory, like the special theory of relativity, does even more for us. Einstein's insight that light moves at the same speed in any inertial frame implies that space, time, and the mass of a moving object contract or expand as a function of the speed with which the object moves relative to a nonaccelerating frame. It is a lens that lets us make a new and valid prediction: the rate at which particles' energy states will decay as a function of the speed with which they move, something the previous picture of space-time did not predict. The new theory does not give us new information. It adds new insight to existing information—to the facts we knew when looking through the old lens—and sets our gaze on critical new information we can seek out.

A new way of looking at a business can also make unseen patterns visible and reveal innovative levers we can use to drive

1

changes that have impact. When Coca Cola describes itself as a conditioned reflex business rather than a "soft drinks business," its marketing department begins to think about how to engineer stimuli that will trigger customers' buy-and-consume routine so reliably that it becomes a reflex. Then the company sets to work on optimizing the color of the drink, the shape of the container, and the sound patterns of the commercials to trigger consumers' desire to "have a Coke and a smile" as a matter of reflex rather than a considered choice.

Google understands itself as a company constantly searching for the best search process. Its approach to research, development, and deployment has taken on a vinelike characteristic—one that is adaptive and expanding. "Search," writ large, is its raison d'être, which encourages it to stay at the forefront of a human activity— search and *re*-search—that has been addictive since before we knew what the Internet was. Google Earth, Google Books, Google Scholar, Google Patents, and Google Code are all exploration vehicles that expand users' search repertoire while furthering the company's own search for better ways to search.

The business world offers up challenges involving large sets of variables on consumer behavior, trends, regulatory uncertainties, shifting competition, new technologies, and more. Finding a way to see these variables in ways that illuminate an insightful course of action is not so different from seeing the world through Bertrand's photo lens or seeing time and space through Einstein's model. The trick is to discover a lens that focuses us on the variables that matter—those we can observe and control to bring about useful change. To do so, we need to look and see differently. We get to insight by building and using a new lens, not just by collecting more data and analyzing it. That is how we design insight.

Shedding new light on a predicament is hard because we tend to gravitate toward familiar ways of seeing. Our existing models, metaphors, and frames shape our ways of looking, and precedents constrain what we end up looking for. They can provide useful shortcuts for transferring insight from one field of practice to another, but they are our enemies in producing new insight: they are the pictures we took using yesterday's lenses.

This book is an exercise regime for the business mind that seeks insight—a personal problem-framing and problem-solving assistant for business problem solvers. It can be used as a think-out-loud document for strategists, advisors, and executives, alone or in teams, and it answers the questions that should guide all insight seekers—for example:

- How can we harness thinking deeply and precisely to seeing more clearly?

- How can we broaden our line of sight into possible solutions—or narrow our focus to avoid getting sidetracked without losing perspective?

- How should we design the process by which we design business solutions?

THE ACT OF DEFINING BUSINESS PROBLEMS: WHERE THE GOLD LIES

In business, we never begin our work with a well-defined problem. We start from a difficulty, an issue, a challenge, or a predicament:

- Quarterly sales have suddenly plummeted. *What now?*

- Manufacturing costs have skyrocketed over the past two quarters. *What do we do about it?*

- Our arch-competitor has announced a new product we'd not even conceived possible a quarter ago, and it looks like a market beater. *How do we respond?*

- The client's top management team has gone into a motivational slump according to the chairman of the board: *How do we change their behavior?*

These are not problems. They are vaguely articulated predicaments, or challenges. As business problem solvers, we never "solve problems" already posed. The work we do creates most of its value through defining problems: turning predicaments into precisely articulated problems we can solve.

What does that mean? What is a well-defined problem? It is a difference between the way things are and the way we want them to be. "Precisely articulated" means just that: we want to be able to measure the most relevant variables pertaining to where we are (the current conditions) and where want to be (the desired conditions); define the time frame in which we will get there from here; and map out the space of possible solutions, that is, the permutations and combinations of all possible changes in the variables we can influence to take us from where we are to where we want to be.

The prototypical well-defined problem is a jigsaw puzzle: you have a stack of nine square tiles, each with some pattern on it. These are the current conditions. You know that the solution to the puzzle is an arrangement of the nine tiles in a square three-by-three tile array such that the patterns fit together, that is, they produce a coherent image (the desired conditions). The space of possible solutions—the solution search space—is all of the possible three-by-three arrays of tiles you can create using the nine tiles at your disposal.

This problem is not simple, but, it is well defined. You know what the solution should look like: you have some hint in or on the box of the tile package. You can verify whether any configuration of tiles fits the bill. You have the means to alter the position or rotation of any tile to get closer to the solution to the puzzle. You may also know that the solution is unique. That will help because you will be aiming to solve for one thing, not for any one of 10, or *100, or 1,000*.

Once you have a well-defined problem, you can write down the full solution search space and the rules for searching for a solution. If you are rushed or derive no enjoyment from solving jigsaw puzzles other than the satisfaction of having solved one, you can hire a good Python or C++ programmer who will, for a hundred dollars or less, write code that finds the solution to the puzzle (and all similar puzzles, to boot) in no more than an hour. Clearly the problem definition step is where the gold lies. It is where we add most value when we are engaged to solve problems. The rest is code.

How do you best turn a loosely, fuzzily, tentatively articulated predicament into a well-defined problem? How do you turn hunches and intimations about difficulties like, "We have an accountability problem around here?" into a problem that is defined in terms of actionable levers and observable inputs and outputs, like, "How do we allocate decision rights over order fulfillment decisions to top management team members to achieve a 20 percent improvement in an accountability metric defined in terms of promises made, kept, and broken, and by the end of six months or sooner?"

"CHERCHEZ LA LANGUE"

Language is the key to defining problems. Language matters to problem solving because it supplies the basis for posing problems, that is, for defining them.

At the core, as businesspeople, we end up truly solving only two kinds of problems: prediction and optimization problems. Prediction problems like these: How will competitors respond to our new product? How will this budget cut affect our ability to ship product next quarter? How will the new management team respond to this new ownership structure? And optimization problems like these: How do we most efficiently increase top-line revenue by 20 percent without making additional investments in sales and marketing? How do we achieve the minimal-cost R&D organization for achieving the desired target for earnings before income, taxes, depreciation, and amortization? How do we most effectively aggregate new client information for maximum informativeness to the top management team so as to cut decision time by 20 percent?

Prediction feels intuitive to us, whereas the concept of optimization *is* worth unpacking because its name and the formalisms that economists and engineers use to represent it often make it sound mysterious and opaque. In fact, it is a natural process that all living creatures engage in at various levels of sophistication, using four elementary steps:

1. Enumerate, or, list, the alternative options for solving a problem. For instance, list all the possible ways to allocate 3 different kinds of incentives to each of 4 different people–already a hefty list of 3^4, or 81, different reward structures.

2. Evaluate the net benefits of each of the alternatives. For instance, evaluate the benefits of the higher motivation induced by the incentives, net of the costs of the side effects of people pursuing their own incentives at the cost of the firm's benefit for each allocation;

3. Compare the net benefits of the different options among them so as to be able to rank them from highest to lowest in terms of the net benefits they will bring.

4. Select the option with the highest net benefit. This is the optimal solution.

Optimization is rarely easy to do. But it is easy to understand and can stay that way if we remember its foundations.

All well-defined business problem are combinations of prediction and optimization problems. The catch-all problem, "What should we do about X?" can always be decomposed into this prediction problem, "What happens if we do a, b, c, and d?" and an optimization problem, "What is the best way to get from X to Y?"

To get to a well-defined prediction-optimization problem requires looking at a challenge through the prism of a problem-solving language. It specifies the variables to try to predict and optimize over, the variables to control and observe, and the measures of performance or success. For example, consider this challenge. The CEO of a large manufacturing business is facing an accountability challenge at the level of her top management team: important client information falls through the cracks, critical orders are shipped late or with defects, and promises that team members make to address the shortfalls are not kept. Order fulfillment is currently slow, sloppy, and unreliable. We can measure speed, precision, and reliability and define an objective—a goal we are driving to. We know the CEO believes the root cause of the difficulty is at the level of the top management team—four executive vice presidents and *chief X officer*-level people whose collective and individual behavior have led us to where we are now. Let's trust her on that (for the time being).

What we do next in this situation depends on the lens we choose, that is, our way of seeing the challenge. It allows us to focus on specific parts of the challenge, which will become the variables of our problem statement. If you look carefully at figure 1.1, you will see that it can turn into a duck head or a rabbit head, depending on where you start off scanning it. Scan it from the left, and it looks like the profile of a duck's head; you will make out the beak, the plumage, and the eye. But scan it from the right, and it looks like the profile of a rabbit's head; you will make out the ears, the fur, and the eye.

Problem-solving languages have the same lensing feature: you can see the challenge as one problem or as another, depending on which language you use. The language is what guides your gaze. For instance, you can think of the team as a network of information flows and trust ties, as figure 1.2 shows. Then you specify the problem in terms of the bottlenecks in the timely and reliable flow of accurate and relevant information about the order fulfillment

FIGURE 1.1.
A bistable image that turns into a duck's head or a rabbit's head, depending on
where your gaze starts scanning. SOURCE: "Kaninchen und Ente" (Rabbit and
duck), *Fliegende Blätter* (October 23, 1892).

process. You next consider ways in which to optimize the network
to minimize bottlenecks, misunderstandings, and the flow of distorted information. You could do this by increasing the flow of information among team members who trust one another or making
public the private exchanges of information between team members who do not trust each other (e.g., using boards that track service levels over time between two production units within a plant),
so distortions of information can be monitored more easily.

Now change your lens and think of the team as shown in figure 1.3: as a group of self-interested agents who make decisions
on the basis of different levels of authority (their decision rights),
different levels of expertise and decision-relevant information,
and their own private incentives that may differ from those of the
business. You can use this to consider ways in which to reallocate
decision rights and incentives to improve the efficiency of the
order fulfillment process—for instance, by giving more decision
rights to team members who have mission-critical information
and aligning the incentives of executives with those of the
business.

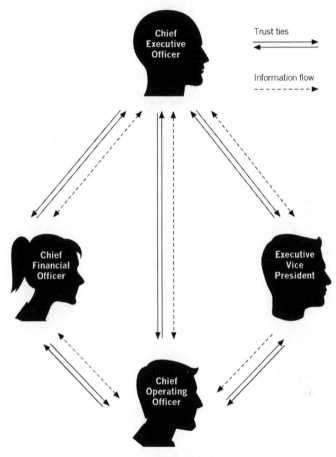

FIGURE 1.2.
Picturing the executive team as an information network.

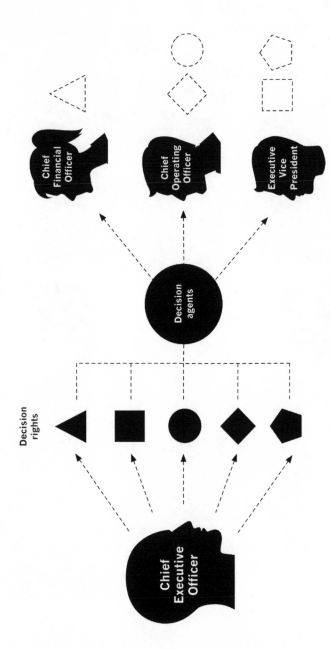

FIGURE 1.3.

Picturing the executive team as a set of agents making mission-critical decisions based on the structure of authority in the team, captured by the distribution of decision rights to team members.

To practice business problem solving effectively, you need a method—a series of reliable steps that prescribe a set of actions and are guided by a goal.

Our method begins by specifying the variables to focus on. If we look at the executive team as a group of agents with different levels of authority, we focus on the relationship between the decentralization of authority (how many decision rights the CEO has relative to others on the team) and the efficiency of the process (orders logged and shipped, delays, defects, rework requests), shown in figure 1.4A. We then estimate from prior experience and industry data the key relationships. Let's say our case studies show that efficiency increases with decentralization of authority for problems such as ours, shown in figure 1.4B. We are on our way to a solution (decentralize authority) except that we do not know where on the curve the current team lies, so we measure the concentration of decision rights in the order fulfillment process in this case, as in figure 1.4C, which gives us the initial conditions for our problem. To figure out what we could do, we use our initial conditions and the relationship between the variables to predict the range of possible improvements we can make, as in figure 1.4D, and then optimize our solution by choosing the allocation of decision rights between top management team members that will produce the greatest improvement in the process measures (fulfillment delays, reliability) in the executive team, as in figure 1.4E).

This five-step process of specify-estimate-measure-predict-optimize (SEMPO) takes us from an ill-defined accountability challenge to a well defined problem (reallocate decision rights over D-type decisions to increase efficiency of process P to which D-type decisions are relevant), which naturally breaks down into two subproblems, predict and optimize, that are the workhorses of business problem solving.

A. What are the relevant variables?

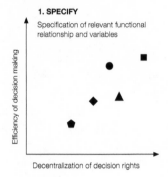

1. SPECIFY

Specification of relevant functional relationship and variables

Efficiency of decision making

Decentralization of decision rights

B. What do we know about the relationship between them?

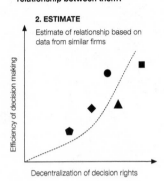

2. ESTIMATE

Estimate of relationship based on data from similar firms

Efficiency of decision making

Decentralization of decision rights

C. Where are we now?

3. MEASURE

Measure of current level of decentralization in target firm

D. Where can we go?

4. PREDICT

Prediction of efficiency increase by decentralizing decision rights

Efficiency of decision making

Decentralization of decision rights

E. How do we get there?

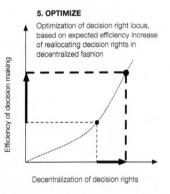

5. OPTIMIZE

Optimization of decision right locus, based on expected efficiency increase of reallocating decision rights in decentralized fashion

Efficiency of decision making

Decentralization of decision rights

FIGURE I.4.

The five elementary components of business problem solving.

What we get by being methodical is depth and precision. We end up with a well-defined, well-posed set of problems we can proceed to solve by making the changes to variables we can measure (decision rights) and that we predict will bring about the desired changes in the values of another set of variables we can measure (efficiency of the order fulfillment process).

Depth of understanding is only one of the upshots of our problem-solving languages. The other is breadth: the diversity that arises from putting several different languages to work on the same challenge.

The "Dream Team"

Imagine you have the chance to build a dream team for competing in a sports meet. You can pick from the 2012 medal winners in all of the sports represented in the Summer Olympic Games to build it: Roger Federer or Andy Murray (tennis, singles), Michael Phelps (swimming), Usain Bolt (short sprint), Sandra Izbasa (gymnastics, vault), Gabby Douglas (gymnastics, parallel bars), and so on. Of course, you will need to compensate each of these athletes according to both the value that he or she brings and each person's market price, so you should choose judiciously.

Your first question may be: What sport am I competing in? It might be inefficient to have both Izbasa and Federer around. Suppose, though, that you do not know in advance what you will have to excel at: you will find out only at the last minute but must commit to a roster now. This may seem unfair, but it is what we have to do when we tackle business problems in real time: we do not know what the world will turn up, but will have to deal with whatever it throws at us. It makes sense, then, to assemble a team that will let you draw on Federer, Bolt, Izbasa, Douglas, and however many more megatalents you can afford, depending on the game you will face. Uncertainty about the game increases the value of your options and flexibility to use them—the value of your team's diversity.

Since you do not know beforehand what talent is needed, you'll want to have as many different talents as possible. That may lead you to build a very expensive team—so expensive, in fact, that the value you might create by winning may be dissipated by the value claimed by the stars you need to keep on retainer. Is there a better way?

There is. You can figure out the skill that each one of the star athletes brings and hire those who bring the highest-value, non-overlapping set of skills to the team. Federer will bring superlative eye-hand coordination: the ability to quickly and forcefully pronate, extend, and supinate the right forearm—essential to the production of his monster forehand—as well as the ability to sprint from a standing start. Bolt will bring height, reach, and an uncanny ability to adduct the hip—the speed-limiting step for a sprinter. Izbasa will bring her spinal flexibility, strength of wrists and ankles, and total body coordination required to land a vault jump without faltering. This basic skill decomposition of each athlete will allow you to make efficient choices in assembling your all-star squad and evaluate the relative and marginal value of any athlete. It seems obvious that you may not need both Federer and Murray but you may also realize that given Federer's skill set, Usain Bolt will be worth less to your endeavor if you've just signed up Federer: you have sprints covered with the Swiss star. That frees up resources to go after other skill sets that do not overlap: maybe you can now afford Kobe Bryant's reach.

The Business Dream Team

If you had to build a dream team of business advisors or executives, your first instinct might be to go for the top experts in the classical functions of business: finance, accounting, marketing, operations, strategy, and human resources management. You do not know beforehand which of these functions will figure prominently in your next assignment, and business problems are not neatly cut up at the joints into parcels that can be dealt with by different experts: you are the one who must do the handiwork of parcellation.

It would be much more efficient if you could identify the elementary skills you would need to solve any business problem and then recruit the team that has the very skills you will require. Strategists and finance theorists may be good at figuring marginal and total incentives and designing value-sharing mechanisms that allow you to extract the maximum benefit from a business situation. Operations specialists may be good at mapping processes in terms of ebbs and flows of raw materials, products on an assembly line, and even money and information.

Each distinctive expertise is in fact based on a problem-solving language spoken by practitioners of a discipline. Like any other languages, these have a vocabulary and a syntax—a bunch of rules for putting words together in phrases. They are also like computer languages in they are used to precisely pose and subsequently solve problems. That is why we call them *problem-solving languages.*

It turns out that most of the languages of business come from just three disciplines—economics, sociology, and psychology—with a few other disciplines, such as operations research, contributing additional models and methods at the margin. Equipped with their basic tool kit of problem-solving languages, you may be able to eschew the experts altogether (along with their inflated fees and self-important talk) and go straight for the core of their expertise. Instead of hiring Federer for his eye-hand coordination, you could hire a nimble juggler with a high willingness to learn new applications of her juggling skill. Or you could design a set of eye-hand coordination exercises that can help one of many more connected, willing-to-help humans produce the performance that you need.

Problem-solving insight itself comes from the diversity of the languages you use to define business problems, which requires mastery of several problem-solving languages. This is a strong claim, and it requires substantiation. A great deal of recent work suggests that teams of smart people from different backgrounds come up with innovative solutions more quickly than individuals or like-minded groups do. The reason is that the individual members of such teams look at predicaments through different lenses, and thus each sees a different problem. Each team member adopts a representation of the problem that is conditioned by her worldview, built out of words and sentences shaped by metaphors or models. A game theorist may articulate the problem of pricing a new product as one of equilibrium calculation and selection. A network theorist may see optimizing strategic partnerships as a problem of choosing the most connected or well-known members of the industry network. A problem of accountability in an organization may look like a pay-for-performance challenge to an economist, whereas the same accountability problem may look to a psychologist like a problem of choosing the management team with the highest individual self-efficacy or the most rooted collective identity.

Team interactions among experts who see problems through different lenses are confrontations among different ways of thinking that force each member to see the problem differently from how he or she would alone. The space of possible solutions grows and more likely will generate the hidden gem of insight because the search is broader and more likely to catch it.

Businesspeople often think of languages as tools for saying stuff, and they are. But they are also tools for seeing and for acting differently: We use language to think, not just to speak. How we think shapes both what we see and what we do. So the language we use shapes how we think and thus what we see and do. Insight is both about seeing more clearly and about seeing more—or seeing what others cannot see. We can get to seeing more by seeing in more ways, which means in different ways:

How Diversity Works

Kevin Dunbar, a cognitive psychologist, studied a number of laboratories to understand how scientists solve problems thrown up by their experimental work. First, he realized that most problems are solved during weekly lab meetings in which scientists describe their experiments and the difficulties they encountered. He then compared the meetings of two teams from different labs who faced the same problem: *Escherichia coli* proteins were sticking to filters, which made them impossible to analyze. He discovered that labs with scientists from different backgrounds (e.g., biochemists, molecular biologists, geneticists, and medical students) generated solutions more quickly than labs with exclusively *E. coli* specialists. "The *E. coli* group took a brute-force approach, spending several weeks methodically testing various fixes. They eventually solved it, but they wasted a lot of valuable time." The more diverse team mulled the problem much longer at each meeting. None of the scientists was a protein expert, so they began a wide-ranging discussion of possible solutions. At first the conversation seemed directionless. But as the chemists traded ideas with the biologists and the biologists bounced ideas off the medical students, potential answers began to emerge. "After another 10 minutes of talking, the protein problem was solved," Dunbar says. "They made it look easy."[1]

Why Diversity Works

Research in a very different field supports Dunbar's conclusions. Mathematical economists Lu Hong and Scott Page have shown analytically that for a complicated problem whose set of possible solutions is so large no expert can find the optimal solution in a finite amount of time, a group of nonexperts will usually outperform a group of experts in solving it.[2] Two conditions apply: everyone understands the problem and can articulate it in his or her own language, and the problem is hard enough that no single expert can solve it using a brute-force approach.

1. Kevin Dunbar, "How Scientists Build Models: In Vivo Science as a Window on the Scientific Mind," in L. Magnani, N. Nersessian, and P. Thagard, eds., *Model Based Reasoning in Scientific Discovery* (New York: Plenum Press, 1999).

2. L. Hong and S. E. Page, "Problem Solving by Heterogeneous Agents," *Journal of Economic Theory* 97 (1): 123–63.

Consider Dunbar's example again. Unlike the *E. coli* experts, the second lab lacked a shared language. In arriving at an understanding of the problem, the team members had to reach for analogies and metaphors to explain things to one another. They introduced one another to different ways of seeing the problem. In contrast, the shared jargon, assumptions, and conventional wisdom led the expert group to shepherd the problem efficiently into a box they all knew how to work in. Unfortunately, the box contained only procedures that were not well tailored to the problem.

To get out of a box, you need different ways of looking at the problem. That's what problem-solving languages give us. But is there a problem-solving language that can be a jack of all trades—one that beats out all others on any problem? It would be nice, but . . .

No Silver Bullet!

Search theory—the theory of optimal search—gives us an answer worth pondering. It was not the case that we would have to think of simultaneously searching for the solution to a problem and for the optimal way to search for a solution to that problem. We would just search for the solution, and solutions that worked in the past would enter folklore, databases, and learned journals. Now, with the proliferation of both memory storage and computational power, we can search for both the best solution *and* the best way to search for the best solution. That is what search theory is all about. David Wolpert, a NASA scientist, recently proved a result that should give pause to any fan of general-purpose silver bullets in problem solving. Using statistical signal processing techniques, he demonstrated there is no problem-solving procedure that beats any other problem-solving procedure on any problem, even if "better" is defined in the average sense. There is no silver bullet.[3] And that

3. D. Wolpert, "No Free Lunch Theorems for Search," NASA Ames Working Paper (1995).

means there is no free lunch either: a problem-solving procedure good enough to solve one tough problem optimally cannot generally be redeployed as is for any other problem.

Once we understand how the language we use shapes how we think, we see why groups of nonexperts or of heterogeneous experts who must develop a broader language just to be able to communicate see a larger solution search space. But these groups also succeed better because of the way they search that space. Intractable problems—the ones that exhaust the calculative abilities of a group searching in a linear, sequential fashion—are always better tackled by randomizing and parallelizing the search for solutions. By putting together a group of heterogeneous problem solvers, we take the first step to being able to randomize our search because each team member will likely proceed differently from the others. In addition, having many team members work on different parts of a problem at the same time can parallelize the search process.

If you are searching for a smart phone lost in a large conference facility, chances are that a combination of different search strategies by starting at different points (entrances, restrooms, presentation venues; searching sequentially by location type or searching in concentric circles around each location) will produce the solution (you are reunited with your smart phone) more quickly than would simply taking a single approach. And taking all of these approaches at the same time—sharing out among many searchers—cuts the time required to find the device.

THE TEMPLATE AND THE LENS: HOW PROBLEM-SOLVING LANGUAGES AND FRAMEWORKS DIFFER

We speak of problem-solving languages as insight generation engines through both precision and diversity. But what exactly is a problem-solving language, and how is it different from a framework?

We'll start from a place we all understand: that of a framework. We all know of some: Five Forces, 7-S, VRIO. Frameworks are templates: they offer fill-in-the-blanks approaches to mapping what we see onto models that others have already built for us. Plug in the numbers, and the framework usually spits out some answer—for example: "Here is your most profitable product market [Five Forces]." "Here is your least imitable source of competitive advantage [VRIO]." Here is your salary competitiveness index in comparison to the rest of your industry [compensation design]."

It's quick and easy but very limiting. The machinery of a framework is fixed, like hardware. There may be sound microeconomic thinking behind the Five Forces framework, for example, but it cannot be adapted to the situation at hand—for instance, examining interactions between the different value chains in an industry, predicting sources of disruptive scalable innovation, or optimizing the strategic planning process within the business at hand. Like the hardware of Apple laptops and iPads, you either use the hardware as is or you buy a new one: you cannot tinker with it. But tinker is what problem solvers to the world need to do to stay adaptive (and alive).

If a framework is a template, a problem-solving language is a lens. Languages can be adapted to a much broader array of problems. They adapt to the situation or challenge we face. The cost of this adaptability is that these languages require fast customization to the situation at hand. We need to translate our predicament into one of these languages: to map firms into agents, decisions, decision rights, incentives, payoffs, and strategies (rational choice theory and game theory), or to map groups of firms into ecologies evolving on the basis of mutation, selection and retention of ideas, technologies, design modules, and best practices (evolutionary theory); or to map teams of top managers into the nodes and edges of an evolving network whose structure is correlated with performance (network theory).

Like frameworks, problem-solving languages have limits: they cannot represent everything. In fact, no single language can even represent everything that can be represented. What can we do about that?

We do what Dunbar's group of nonexperts did: replace one problem-solving language with two or more. Two is more than twice as valuable as one, and three are more than three times as valuable. Then we take a page from the logic of evolutionary mechanisms and engage in recombinant problem shaping. Thinking of an organization as a set of games played among self-interested strategic agents *and* as a network of relationships that embeds and constrains their actions helps us to focus on both the bargaining power of team members and on their affective, informational, and power relationships. Thinking of a consumer as an organism who has stimulus-triggered, experience-conditioned responses that are prone to marketing influences *and* as a decision agent capable of rational choices based on internal deliberation regarding costs and benefits focuses us on both the immediate and possibly subconscious causes of her behavior *and* on her conscious reasons for choosing our client's product over that of the competition. Thinking of an assembly line as a computer carrying out a calculation that converges to an answer when the finished product leaves the assembly line with zero defects *and* as a networked group of workers whose productivity changes as a function of the pattern of information flow within their network along high-trust links and bridges focuses us on both the structure of the tasks that the line performs *and* on the relations among the humans performing those tasks. Thinking of an industry as a set of profit-maximizing agents (firms) that compete with one another on price and quality by making proactive and deliberate changes to their products, cost structures, pricing policy, quantity commitments, distribution networks, and marketing and R&D investments *and* as an ecology of organisms that compete for survival by making a myriad random, often unplanned point changes to their structure and function allows us to focus on both the strategic and operational choice and option set of a firm in that industry and on its unplanned and uncharted behavioral and structural blueprint, as sources of advantage.

A combination of problem-solving languages mimics the diversity of Dunbar's nonexpert group. It replicates at the level of business problem-solving prowess the skill set of the Olympic dream team we had fantasized about assembling. Now all we have to do is to choose which problem-solving languages to master.

Crafting Internal Diversity

We are often not in a position to build a diverse team of problem solvers by accessing disparate pools of experts who must often be trained to collaborate with one another and overcome significant ego-related counterproductive ways of being before cooperatively producing insight. The alternative to sourcing native speakers of different problem-solving languages is to build our own internal collection of problem-solving languages, for any group of mentally agile people trained to use them can serve as a substitute for the wisdom and experience of a diverse experts in this case.

However, the world is full of languages. Which to choose, and why?

David Deutsch, a quantum theorist moonlighting as an epistemologist, gives us a useful hint. In *The Fabric of Reality*, he starts by bemoaning the loss of the Renaissance man—an Empedocles, a Leonardo, a Galileo, a Vico, a Goethe, a Hegel, a Leibniz, that is, a person who "understands everything"—in the age of hyperinformation, hypercomputation, and hyperspecialization.[4] Folk wisdom has it that no one in this day and age can even hope for, let alone attain, an understanding of everything in the natural and social sciences. There are too many specialized terms of art, too much technical detail, too much know-how that a single mind

4. D. Deutsch, *The Fabric of Reality* (New York: Penguin, 1997).

would have to master to solve problems that may arise from any and all domains of human activity.

But Deutsch realizes that a global and transcendental understanding is possible: one *can* understand everything, if by "everything" we mean "everything that can be understood." The key is to possess a special, core set of languages that are the modern equivalent of the philosopher's stone, that is, the object that allows its beholder access to the darkest mysteries of the world. Deutsch's candidates for this small set of languages are quantum mechanics, information theory, evolutionary theory, and the theory of computation. What they have in common is a curious property called logical depth: deep languages explain a lot with a little. They start from a small, sparse, widely applicable assumption base and produce explanations and predictions of massively complex phenomena—of giga-, tera-, or peta-bytes of data.

What more can you ask for? Master these languages, and you will have access to the treasure troves of knowledge and expertise that range from chemistry to botany, from aeronautical engineering to soil science, and from the design of new ontologies for database management to the implementation of expert systems for playing chess, Nintendo, or your favorite mind game. Master their vocabulary and syntax—the way you put their specialized terms together in meaningful sentences—and you will be able to "understand everything that can be understood": there is no publication or research report or review article, no matter how complicated or esoteric, that you will not be able to decode and make sense of.

Why the Philosopher's Stone Is Not Enough

"Not bad!" you might say. "Why not, then, just use these languages and be done with it? Why do we not just learn quantum mechanics, evolutionary theory, and information and computation theory, and dispense with the minutiae of our accumulated knowledge and expertise base in various industries and disciplines?"

There are two reasons. First, *problem solving is not a spectator sport.* Deutsch is on a quest to understand, not to predict, control, and interact with the object of his understanding. His languages, though useful, are passive. They are far more useful to the scientist-philosopher who, like the Renaissance scientist, is interested in observation and analysis than to the person of action. Second, *language is a tool for doing, not just for seeing and saying.* Deutsch's languages live far away from practical reality, which is different from empirical reality because it confronts you with a problem to solve and a time frame to solve it within. You have to do a lot of work to generate useful predictions and explanations of any system you care about using information theory alone: conceptual work, computational work, experimental work, and so on. Deutsch's languages are highly useful as decoders of the increasingly abstruse knowledge base of science because they are computationally very complex.

So Deutsch's philosopher's stone is not enough because we are not just philosophers! We cannot stop where Deutsch does because his languages are merely descriptive.

What We Need of Our Languages

We are after problem-solving languages that offer guidance for immediate action and let us build solution search spaces for business challenges as they happen. Here, then, is what the languages we'll build require for them to be useful.

Actionability

Languages can be used to quickly map the business predicaments we face into inputs (or independent variables), outputs (or dependent variables), and levers (or structural variables we can change in order to modify the outputs given a series of inputs). Take our decision agent language. It posits that incentives, decision rights, and levels of expertise and information are inputs that we can observe and measure, and levels of performance is an output that we can observe and measure. It also lets us play with the allocation of decision rights and incentives—the levers—in ways that are likely to produce changes in the desired levels of accountability (the outputs).

Our networks language does the same. It lets us map the patterns of relations among the members of a top management team (whether they be trust, information exchange, interactional ties, or something else) and attempt to change some of these relations (our levers for changing the topology of the network) in order to produce greater levels of team and individual accountability. These examples demonstrate the first requirement of a problem-solving language: it gives us observable, measurable, and controllable variables, along with a set of hypotheses that link the input to the output variables via levers we can access.

Versatility

Our problem-solving languages must be applicable at many levels of analysis in a business. Each can be applied at the level of individuals, teams, firms, markets, institutions, and even societies and world systems taken as a whole. Once we understand the way the decision agent language works, we can speak of individuals, teams, and institutions as a whole as agents and examine their utilities and preferences, decision rights, beliefs, strategies, levels of specific knowledge, and incentives. This is an enormously important feature because it allows us to tailor and adapt our problem-solving language to a large number of different situations and predicaments without making radical changes to the syntax or semantics of the language in question. Due to the flexibility of our problem-solving languages, we call them *flexons: flexible objects for generating of novel solutions.*

Compactness

A problem-solving language should capture a lot with a little. The explanatory engine of classical mechanics is sparse. Newton's three laws of motion, the law of universal gravitation, and two conservation principles—for momentum and energy—form perhaps the densest explanatory core of all the sciences. As another example, the basic building blocks of evolutionary theory—selection, variation, retention—are all we need to describe industries as population ecologies of firms, which in turn are population ecologies of people, technologies, strategies, or any other entity striving to survive.

THE FIVE FLEXONS AT A GLANCE

With these requirements in mind, we realized we needed to reach beyond the traditional disciplines of business. We scoured the modeling tool kits of both the social and natural sciences to distill out five problem-solving languages that fit them. They are:

1. The *networks flexon*, which uses nodes, ties that connect them, and the distribution and topology of these ties as a basic set of causally relevant variables

2. The *decision agent flexon*, which uses decision agents and their decision rights, incentives, beliefs, and knowledge states as a basic set of causally relevant variables

3. The *system dynamics flexon*, which uses causally linked variables, like matter or money that flow and can accumulate, and passive components, like resistors and capacitors, as a basic set of relevant variables

4. The *evolutionary flexon*, which uses parent offspring populations of entities that compete for survival, along with mechanisms of variation, selection, and retention as a basic set of relevant variables

5. The *information processing flexon*, which uses problem-solving agents (entities capable of storing and processing information) and the processes they use to solve problems as a basic set of causally relevant variables

The balance of this book is dedicated to showing how each these five flexons can be used to define and structure the challenges and predicaments the business world throws our way into well-defined problems we can solve in practice. What follows is a crash course in the use of these flexons to turn loosely structured business predicaments and situations into precisely articulated business problems. Its intended outcome is a brand-new skill that enables readers to picture the world in several different ways corresponding to different flexons and to switch between different pictures in order to engineer new insights that could not have been generated through the use of one problem-solving language alone.

IF YOU WANT MORE

For a panoptic view of explanatory and predictive models across scientific disciplines and branches of philosophy, see:

Deutsch, D. (1997). *The Fabric of Reality*. New York: Penguin.

For a model-centric exploration of the patterns and processes of what we call thought, see:

Hofstadter, D. O. (1978). *Godel, Escher, Bach: An Eternal Golden Braid*. New York: Basic Books.

Hofstadter, D. O. (1993). *Fluid Concepts and Creative Analogies: Computer Models of the Fundamental Mechanisms of Thought*. New York: Basic Books.

For an exposition of representational structures (models) used to structure perception and reasoning, see:

Johnson-Laird, P. M. (1991). *Mental Models*. Cambridge, MA: Harvard University Press.

For a view of problem-solving processes as algorithms and heuristics applied to well defined-problems across fields, see:

Michalewicz, Z., and D. B. Fogel. (1999). *How to Solve It: Modern Heuristics*. New York: Springer.

For an inquiry into successful patterns of thinking and behaving informed by algorithm and heuristic design and performance analysis, see:

Moldoveanu, M. C., and R. L. Martin. (2009). *Diaminds: Decoding the Mental Habits of Successful Thinkers*. Toronto: University of Toronto Press.

2 THE NETWORKS FLEXON

As the head of marketing and sales for a multibillion-dollar phar-maceuticals company, C. Marie Ofisser was tasked with accelerat-ing the market uptake of a new drug approved by the Food and Drug Administration used to treat a chronic disease. Human trial results had exceeded expectations in both the size of the treatment effect and the occurrence of anticipated side effects, and the com-pany expected market response would be overwhelmingly posi-tive. However, in spite of several months of intensive marketing and sales activity, sales of the drug were stagnant. Ofisser had con-structed a map of who makes what decisions in new drug acquisi-tions in hospitals, clinics, and health maintenance organizations (HMOs) and found there is a group of physician-researchers and hospital and HMO executives whose recommendations and be-havior were highly correlated with the widespread use of any new drug in this clinical domain. She realized that influencing the in-fluencers was the best way for the company to pursue the relaunch of the drug. However, she also quickly discovered that these gate-keepers were loath to engage in conversations with pharmaceuti-cals representatives and cherished their clinical independence. What to do?

Ofisser figured out that although this group was impervious to outside persuasion and influence, it was very much susceptible to influence from inside. Clinicians made decisions on the basis of recommendations of other clinicians or researchers whom they had interacted, transacted, or collaborated with. The key to mapping out the influence flows within the group was to think of it as a network of professional and personal relationships, which her team reconstructed from citation (Who cites whom?), co-citation (Who publishes with whom?), collaboration (Who uses whose data?), and communication (Who shows up with whom at professional and academic conferences?).She quickly mapped out the three networks and found significant overlap between them. She then correlated these networks with pharmacoclinical recommendation patterns and found that institutional, research, and professional affiliation were highly correlated with coincidence of therapeutic agent recommendations. She realized it was not individual hospital and HMO executive teams she should try to focus on and not individual clinicians and care providers who provided for patients diagnosed with the condition but, rather, the network of physician scientists and researchers who acted as experts.

Given these individuals' incentives were difficult to change, she focused the division's marketing efforts toward building connections between researcher-clinicians who had seen the benefits of the new drug and those who either were not aware of the drug's existence or benefits or were misinformed about its benefits. She proceeded to organize, support, and synchronize a series of webinars, conferences, gatherings, and clinical symposia that aimed to bring together disparate cliques and subgroups in the larger network, aimed at strengthening the network's informational conductivity about the benefits of the new drug. She also focused her marketing efforts on the most-connected and the best-connected (those most connected to the well connected) researchers and clinicians in order to maximize the penetration of information and influence in the network. In hindsight, it was a winning strategy brought about by a shift in the lens through which Offiser viewed the situation: not formal organizations governed by executive-dominated hierarchies with information flowing upward and decisions flowing downward and decisions being made on the basis of clearly defined incentives. Rather, there would be networks—and lots of them, both formal and informal—of researcher clinicians for whom their position in the network is far more important than hierarchical authority and compensation.

Welcome to the networks flexon! Its intellectual heritage cuts across many well-known and well-used disciplines: the application of network models in explaining and predicting behavior in interpersonal (Who likes whom? Who dates whom? Who trusts whom?) and interorganizational networks (Who trades with whom? Who collaborates with whom?); networks of web pages (Which page is most cited?), data mining (What covaries with what?), as well as the optimization of traffic (minimize delays) and communications (maximize reliability). Network models and the methods for using them form a stand-alone business problem-solving language.

To see how the networks flexon works, we need to view any business entity, ranging from a team or group to a market or an institution, in relational terms, as a nexus of nodes (people, groups, firms) and connections. Then questions like the following that will come to mind:

- *Who is related to whom, and in what way?* This allows us to specify the components of the network—the nodes and the ties;

- *What difference to the behavior of a team, a person, or a business do differences in connections make?* This allows us to estimate the effects of the network's structure on the variables we want to change;

- *How do we change the behavior of the business by changing the structure of the network?* This allows us to make predictions about changes in behavior and performance we can hope to achieve and to optimize the network for our purpose.

A new prism takes shape: a language for defining the problems we want to solve. As with any other language, we need to build a lexicon, which we do by asking, What is the network? This question in fact needs to unpacked so we get a sense of the nature of the nodes and the connections between them. So:

The first thing we ask is, "What are the nodes–in other words, the basic entities in terms of which we build out our network?" They could be people, groups, teams, firms, things, facts, products, product modules. . . .

Second, "What is the nature of the connections between the nodes, that is, the links between the nodes?" They can be used to represent frequency of interactions among people, buyer-seller relationships among firms, trust ties, friendship ties, information flows within groups, teams and whole organizations, logical entailment relationships among different clauses in a patent application, and so forth. We can choose the type of tie that is most relevant to the predicament—for example, trust ties and information flows in an executive team, logical relationships among the claims of a patent application, travel routes for an airline in North America, patterns of exchange in a vertically disintegrated industry, deal flows in the pipeline of a private equity firm. Networks, networks everywhere!

The last question is, "What kinds of connections are they?" You will notice that not all connections are the same. Some are directed. These are one-way: node 1 → node 2). For example, information regarding sales quota achievement may flow from the vice president of sales and marketing to the CEO, but not vice versa. It may also flow between the directors of sales in various operational theaters and the vice president of sales and marketing, but not vice versa. The vice president may consider himself to be the CEO's friend, but not vice versa. The client may purchase raw materials from a third party, but not vice versa. In these cases, we use directional ties to fill in the network connectivity map. Other ties are not directed (i.e., node 1—node 2). If Alice interacts with Bob twenty-one times a day, then Bob also interacts with Alice twenty-one times a day.

Connections also differ with regard to their strength. Some executives in a top management team interact more frequently with one another than do others. Some product modules are strongly connected to other modules, so changing one requires a change in the other modules too, for instance. Others are less well connected: changing them only facilitates changes in other modules. Some trading relationships among countries are more intensive; others are less so. To capture tie strengths, we can use numerical weights that index the strength of each connection.

To keep things precise, we specify a different network every time we change nodes or their connections, or both. Consider the executive team with five people shown in figure 2.1:

- An interaction network that is undirected and weighted (Who interacts with whom, and how frequently?)

- A friendship network that may be directed (Who says what about who on the team is her friend?)

- A trust network (Who trusts whom with sensitive information?)

- A collaboration network (Who has worked with whom on specific company-wide projects in the past?)

Just the act of mapping these networks and creating a "network X-ray" of the team gives insight into its workings.

▶ YOU MIGHT WISH TO CONSIDER . . .

How would you use the network flexon to model—by specifying the nodes and the nature and distribution of the ties of the network—the following groups and gatherings:

- The set of airline hubs in the European Union?

- Your last working group?

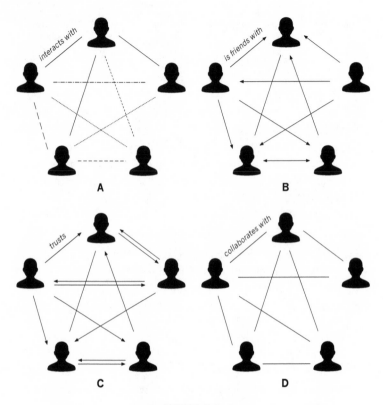

FIGURE 2.1.
Different types of networks that can exist among five people, characterized by different definitions of the links: interactions (A), friendship (B), trust (C), and collaboration (D).

- The set of modules making up the latest version of a smart phone?

- The set of activities in a surgical operating room?

- The value-linked activity chain of the last industry you worked in?

- The flow of ideas in your last problem-solving session?

.   .   .

Mapping out the network is only the first part of the specification job. We also need to figure out what it is about the network that matters—in other words, which of its properties will we focus on.

One set of measures has to do with how efficient the network is at conducting information and enabling coordination. To get a sense of how different networks do this, consider trying to increase the efficiency of the process by which a top management team makes product launch decisions. For example, suppose we think that information flows more freely between people when they interact more frequently and that more information flow will lead to more informed decisions. That means we can distinguish among management teams' informational efficiency on the basis of differences in the topology of their interaction networks.

The interaction networks of four different management teams are mapped out in figure 2.2. The first team (figure 2.2a) has a center-periphery structure: the CEO is at the center. That could work well if the CEO is transparent and fully trusted by her executive team members: it saves on communication costs because everyone conveys information directly to the CEO and trusts she will heed it. However, if the team does not trust the CEO, the pattern of information flows this network generates is one in which some executive team members hoard information, thus keeping it private, or, even worse, they distort it when they communicate it to the CEO to bias her decisions favorably. Valuable information is thus lost or distorted.

Our second team's network (figure 2.2b) is a pure circle: each executive interacts with two others and no more. Each, including the CEO, is a bridge between two other executives. In this network, there are opportunities galore for information loss and distortion because the CEO has a local and limited view of what his executive team thinks and does, and any one executive can, even if only unwittingly, distort information passed on to her when she relays it to a colleague.

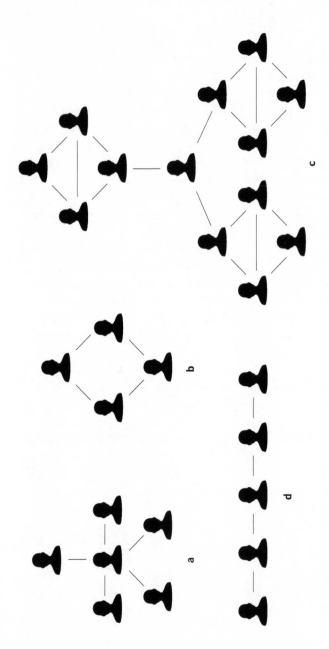

FIGURE 2.2.

Different structures of the interaction network of four top management teams.

The third team's network X-ray (figure 2.2c) shows a set of sparsely connected cliques featuring dense connections among small subnetworks of executives. Executives in the same clique trust each other, so information here flows freely. However, executives belonging to different cliques do not. The cliques become factions, and deliberation processes become political: arguments pro and con are presented by each faction in a biased, distorted, contentious, and tendentious fashion with a view solely to advancing its own interest.

Our fourth team (figure 2.2d) is a straight line. It has all of the properties of poor information relay of the circle and no termination point—someone who may at least function as a feedback node for information distortion or loss. The CEO thus has a local and restricted view of information flows. This can cause his decisions to be strategically myopic because they are biased by the information passed on to him by the two executives he interacts and exchanges information with.

We have taken the word *efficiency* and gotten precise about its meaning by building a network model of information transmission within executive teams. We measure the network through interviews and questionnaires and build out a network picture of information flows on the executive team. Then we zero in on the specific losses and distortions of information that the structure of the network likely leads to and propose changes to the network structure that will produce an improvement—for instance:

- Close up the untethered line network at the bottom of figure 2.2 by promoting interactions between the two endpoint executives to introduce a useful self-correction loop on the spread of rumors and hearsay.

- Break up the executive cliques at the top middle position by changing the office locations of the executive team or facilitate bridges across the cliques by having regular meetings of groups of people drawn from different cliques.

- Make relevant information centrally available and auditable to build trust by increasing transparency in the hub-and-spokes network at the top left with a common agenda and publicly available meetings for each strategic or operational meeting.

▶ YOU MIGHT WISH TO CONSIDER . . .

What was the information network structure of your last working group? What are the possible sources of efficiency loss this structure entails? How can you improve the efficiency of that group by making changes to its information network structure?

.   .   .

There is value in simply visualizing a team or firm as a network because we can't otherwise see cliques and gaps. In a distributed, multiregional organization, we posit that efficiency failures often arise from distorted and hoarded information, which arises from trust gaps. Then we correlate the trust networks with the geographical co-location network and figure out whether people in the same office are more or less likely to trust one another. We correlate information bottlenecks and coordination failures that have led to mishaps, crises, or even debacles in the business and figure out who the people involved were and their position in the network (Were they well connected? Were they in a clique?). We then propose measures for changing the structure of the network, for example, with geographical moves or promotions (demotions) of people who are trusted (untrusted) to increase its efficiency.

If we view the organization as a large information network, we can examine the structure of that network with a view to increasing its informational effectiveness. Global measures of the network are then proxies and measures of the efficiency of the business. The average connectedness of a manager (the average number of connections that each manager has to others in the network) lets us measure the density of the network. The distribution of the connectivity of the people in the network (from least connected to most connected) gives us a measure of who is connected, how well connected the well connected are, and how many well-connected people there are. The informational path length of the network—the average number of nodes a piece of critical information must pass through to go from one person to any other person—gives us a sense of how responsive the business is likely to be to strategically or operationally relevant information.

The flexon lets us see what was previously invisible or fuzzy: the network structure of the business, which shapes and constrains the ways and paths by which information flows and enable the design of business-wide initiatives. An example is creating cross-regional, cross-functional teams that are specifically designed to accomplish a strategically important objective and improve the efficiency of the business by modifying the structure of its information exchange networks.

INFORMATION POWER AND MONOPOLY POWER: POSITIONAL ADVANTAGE AND THE STRATEGIC USE OF THE NETWORK FLEXON

We use the networks flexon not only to optimize topologies of teams, business, and even markets, but also to optimize node-level properties, like the monopoly power, connectedness, and the reputation of a person, a team, or a business. Seen through a network lens, power and influence have a precise interpretation: Whom do you know, who knows you, how well known are those who know you, and how much better are you on these measures than others in the same network? As soon as we figure out what the network is and what value social capital—or network position—has to the node we are interested in, we can design ways of increasing that power by making changes to the connectivity of the node.

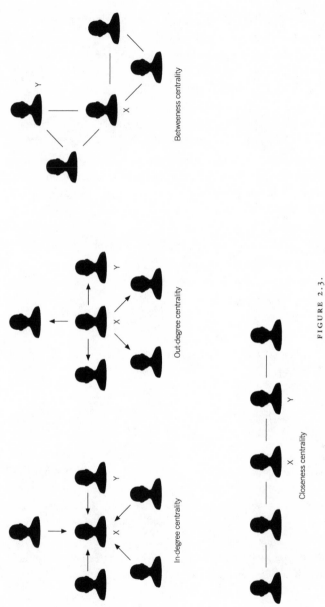

FIGURE 2.3.

Different networks flexons representations of the importance of a node.

How important a node is depends on what kind of network it is in and how it is connected to other nodes. Look at the two people, X and Y, in the four information-interaction networks of figure 2.3. In each case, person X is more important than Y, but in each network, "more important" has a different meaning.

In the first network (upper left of figure 2.3), X has more information paths going into him than does Y, and hence has greater *in-degree centrality*. In the second network (upper right), X has more information paths going out of her than does Y and hence has a greater *out-degree centrality*. In the third network (lower left), there are more paths connecting remote people in the network going through X than there are going through Y and, hence, a greater *betweenness centrality*. In the fourth network (lower right), X is closer to more people in the network than is Y and, hence, has a greater *closeness centrality*.

Suppose we want to figure out why the deal flow at Money Masters (MM) LLP, a private equity fund specializing in management and leveraged buyouts of scalable, cash-flow-neutral-to-positive companies in technology-intensive service and product businesses. MM has $20 billion under management. There are myriad variables we can look at to examine their effects on fund performance, including across-industry life cycles—economic booms and busts, technology bulls and bears—and across the various target industries MM plays in. However, there is no guarantee that what has worked in the past for MM and in other industries for other funds will work here. Not only does correlation not entail causation, but the longitudinal and cross-sectional data do not give us enough precision to articulate why certain strategies worked and others did not. The networks flexon allows us to drill down and build a precise model of this situation by focusing on MM as a node in multiple networks: co-investment (other funds), those in strategic acquisition, underwriters, investment bankers and brokers, venture lenders and venture capitalists, target industries, and technology sources (research labs, universities).

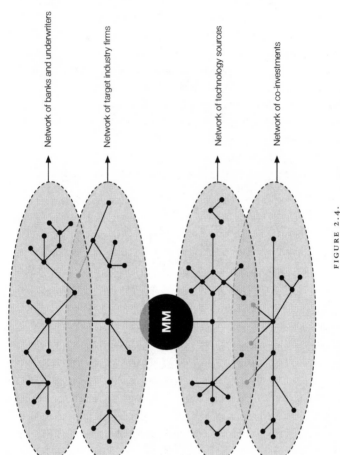

Network of banks and underwriters

Network of target industry firms

Network of technology sources

Network of co-investments

MM

FIGURE 2.4.

Mapping MM's position in the multiple informational networks it belongs to.

Each network MM operates in has different implications for its network capital, or position. In some networks, it pays to know lots of players, as is the case with networks of technology sources and entrepreneurial teams. In other networks, like that of investment bankers, status is the key: being known by well-known players will be a good leading indicator of success. In still other networks , like coinvestment and syndication networks, it is being in the deal flow that counts, which means being part of the paths connecting the key players in the network. With the map of MM's networks in hand in figure 2.4, we can get precise about the positional advantage of MM in its networks and guide MM's partners on their networking strategy .

- *Degree centrality*. In networks of technology sources and entrepreneurial teams where the distribution of value is highly unpredictable, it pays for MM to know lots of players. Its degree centrality captures how richly connected it is relative to other funds by measuring the number of players it is connected to relative to all of the players it could be connected to.

- *Betweenness centrality*. In networks like those of coinvestment and syndication networks of funds or deal flow networks like those comprising companies and underwriters, it pays for MM to be in between as many players as possible, that is, on the shortest network path connecting them. Its betweenness centrality captures the likelihood that the shortest path through the network that connects one node to others needs to pass through MM and measures its informational advantage.

- *Closeness centrality*. In networks like those of firms in target industries that may seek access to capital by word-of-mouth recommendations from within-industry trusted sources, it pays for MM to be close to a lot of firms. Its closeness centrality is a measure of its relative proximity to all of the players in the target network.

- *Eigenvector centrality.* In networks where social capital is highly correlated with *knownness* or *status*, like that of investment bankers and underwriters, it will pay for MM to be recognized (i.e., referenced, quoted, known) by high-status players. MM's eigenvector represents its status by measuring how connected it is to other well-connected players.

We now have a complete composite of MM's social capital measures and precise ways of calculating them that allows us to figure out:

- What partnerships MM should form to increase its relevant centrality measure in the networks it plays in. The advantage of a precise measure applied to a given network is that for each new connection formed, we can predict the centrality advantage it will bring.

- What ties MM should sever in order to increase its relevant centrality measure

- Whether there are any ties between other nodes that MM should think of trying to sever in order to improve its network position

- What communication strategies (e.g., channels, targets) MM should use to increase its centrality measures in the target networks. We can use network centrality measures as outcome measures and proxies for the effectiveness of MM's strategic communications.

CHALLENGE

The client firm is a large pharmaceuticals company with dominant market share in several therapeutic agents. It faces declining revenue from the existing product base and short time lines until the expiration of patent protection afforded to its core products. It is also facing a decline in the productivity of its research and development team and looking for a short-term solution to boosting sales of existing products and a long-term solution to increasing the productivity of its research and development team.

Specify

We specify the nodes of the network to be that of physicians and researchers in the field who act as influencers of prescription choices and lead developers of new therapies, drugs, and drug precursors. We next specify the ties among them to be collaboration ties, and measure these by co-authorship and co-citation. These ties will also proxy for high levels of interaction and mutual trust. We specify two measures for the network at two levels. One is the average degree and closeness centrality of the nodes, which will measure the spread of innovation from one location in the network to another. The other is the specific degree and closeness centrality of the physicians and researchers who are the specific promoters of the client's pharmaceutical and therapeutic innovations. We specify the betweenness centrality of agents in the network as a measure of the degree to which some physicians are catalysts of the introduction of new therapies and new innovations because they broker information across different research and therapeutic centers. We specify a set of actionable levers for making changes in the structure of the network and the position of relevant agents, conditional on the tie formation and dissolution mechanisms or rules that the network agents use. They may take the form of new online and conference forums for sharing and pooling information (proximity-based association), new collaborative research grants aimed at maximizing connectivity among disjoint cliques of researchers (preferential attachment and strategic association mechanisms), new databases that reward information sharing with real-time access to research findings before publication or public release, and new specific challenge sites and platforms that encourage real-time collaboration on problems that are at the core of the development process.

Estimate

We estimate the relationships between our postulated variables (network topology and the position of central agents) and performance measures such as the influence of central agents on resource allocation decisions, information spread, and speed of innovation. Wherever we do not have sufficient data to estimate these relationships, we try to match the topology of the network and the position of the focal agents (the ones we can influence) to the function of the network and the network capital or influence of the node to produce sensible estimates and extrapolations.

Measure

We now measure the network: the specific agents and their co-authorship and co-citation patterns; the distribution of ties; the degree of the betweenness and closeness centrality of the individual physicians and researchers in the network; and the current performance levels. We specify a performance improvement target for the network as a whole: revenue increase due to higher adoption rates, patent application rates, and new articles published in a core set of journals.

Predict

We make predictions about the effects of modifications in the topology of the network and the position of the focal nodes on the performance measures we have selected. We may predict, for instance, that increasing the degree centrality of five key physician scientists by 20 percent could lead to an increase in adoption rates for the new drugs and therapies of the client of 10 percent over two years. Or we may predict that developing bridges between the subnetwork of promoters and three key cliques in the network that are currently unaligned can lead to an increase in greenfield users of the therapies enabled by the client's drugs of 40 percent over a year.

Optimize

We evaluate and rank alternative network topology and node position changes with respect to their predicted effects on performance measures and select the most promising approaches for implementation. We use the network model that the application of the flexon has produced to simulate possible alternatives and figure out what would likely happen if we tried one way or another to change the structure of the network in order to improve its performance for the client.

FOR FUN AND PRACTICE: MORE CHALLENGES

1. A multinational software company had hundreds of development centers worldwide. The distributed team found it challenging to collaborate effectively and efficiently, with the result that product development time was long and costs high. Product managers were increasingly frustrated with the results. Team members' location in different time zones and continents—even teams in the same location in different buildings—made it hard to efficiently conduct basic requirements gathering, development, and testing. The client asked for help in identifying ways in which the development team could increase its efficiency and adopt more productive protocols.

2. A major sports league was experiencing wide variability in the performance of its digital properties, including uneven levels of traffic to the websites of different teams and visibility on "earned media" platforms such as Facebook and Twitter. The league asked for help in evaluating objectively each team's online practices and identify new opportunities, even for its best-performing team sites, by looking at other leading sports sites as well as the overall digital media landscape.

3. A leading nonfood retailer was spending a significant share of its revenues on market communication, especially on classical advertising. Executives at the company were uncertain about the value they were getting and asked for help in evaluating the size of the company's total marketing budget, how effectively spending was allocated to different media, and how marketing efforts were influencing the consumer-purchase funnel.

IF YOU WANT MORE: ANNOTATED BIBLIOGRAPHY

For a pedagogical introduction to the use of network analysis for human networks, see:

Faust, K., and J. Wasserman. (1994). *The Analysis of Social Networks*. Cambridge: Cambridge University Press.

For a transdisciplinary account of the use of networks as general purpose models, see:

Barabasi, A.-L., and R. Albert. (2002). "The Statistical Mechanics of Complex Networks." *Reviews of Modern Physics* 74:47–97

For an expanded account of the use of network analysis across different fields, see:

Newman, M. J. (2011). *Networks*. Princeton, NJ: Princeton University Press.

For an economic approach to social networks, see:

Jackson, M. (2008). *Social Networks: An Economic Approach*. Princeton, NJ: Princeton University Press.

For an extension of network analysis to the role of beliefs and perceptions of networked human agents on the structure and dynamics of the network and on the flow of information in networks see:

Moldoveanu, M. C., and J.A.C. Baum. (2013). *Epinets: The Epistemic Structure and Dynamics of Social Networks*. Stanford, CA: Stanford University Press.

3   THE DECISION AGENT FLEXON

Cy O. Ough had been given the immediate task of improving the efficiency of the logistics and distribution network as the chief operating officer of a consumer goods multinational, a network through which some $8 billion of goods and materials flowed annually. In this network were suppliers, buyers, shipping companies, warehousing companies, distributors and channel partners, and thousands of end users and end user agents who issued orders on fulfillment deadlines ranging from days to years. The imperative to optimize distribution arose from a study that showed the company was lagging behind best practices in the industry and from cost pressure the business was feeling from new competitors. The distribution network looked like a labyrinth: thousands of destinations and flows of goods connecting them in a dynamically evolving network.

There are myriad ways to improve this network. Where to start? More important, how could Cy figure out which new configurations would be more promising? But Cy was resourceful. He knew he wanted a way to cut through the complexity of a massive network and find the set of small differences that would make a really big difference. He figured out that the top five clients and the top ten distributors accounted for more than 70 percent of the flow of goods and money through the mega-network. If he could only come up with a way of increasing price-cost margins for this core, a path to a solution would be at hand. To do this, he had to let go of his typical operations perspective on the distribution and order fulfillment network and carefully think about the decisions that the suppliers and distributors in the select group were making: what they were driven by and what the decision makers valued. He visited them, asked them, and spent time trying to understand their preferences. He learned they would be willing to pay much more for decreasing the variance in order fulfillment by as little as 20 percent. And they would be willing to absorb some of the costs of inventory in exchange for an interface that allowed them to track the specifics of their orders. Rather than seeing them as passive nodes in a network where only distances and geodesics mattered to the overall cost structure, the new lens led Cy to pose a different problem—one that yielded a high-impact solution.

DECISIONS AND THE ENTITIES THAT MAKE THEM: THE DECISION AGENT FLEXON

A business is a massively complex object. To understand it, we must decompose it in terms of a set of entities we can adjust or change in order to improve performance, which is exactly what a flexon is designed to do. The decision agent flexon is a problem-solving language that functions as an imaging tool for framing challenges in terms of decisions and those who make them (the decision agents), along with their decision rights, incentives, expertise, information, and performance measures.

Even what seems like a simple business—say, a multiregional, multiple-outlet fashion retailer—is massively complicated: it is very difficult to have an impact on its evolution in a positive and lasting fashion by purposively changing it. When the challenge is to increase productivity or profitability or identify opportunities for changing cost structure through the intelligent use of technology, deciding where to start is always the greatest hurdle. Just like a cartographer sent off to the farthest reaches of the world to build a map of the terrain that others can use to guide their trips and treks, the business problem solver must decide on the basic set of objects to represent the situation. The cartographer armed with a simple lexicon (mountains, valleys, plains) will not be able to distinguish among different types of elevations (hills, peaks, ranges) or among different types of flatlands (deserts, steppes, tundras), that require him to make additional distinctions that are not in the basic lexicon.

Consider our retailer at the start of the chapter as an example. The flexon supplies a basic kit of entities: decisions made by decision agents in ways that differ according to their decision rights, incentives, expertise, and information and have consequences begetting costs and benefits to both the decision agents and the organization. We use it to build a basic map of the retailer efficiency optimization problem by first choosing the decision agents we want to focus on (department store, headquarters managers, and employees), the decisions that are made, and the information and knowledge that is needed to make each decision. The resulting map in figure 3.1 should allow us to figure out both who makes what decisions and who should make each decision because they have information relevant to it.

Our efficiency optimization problem can now be posed in sharper terms: Do the people with unique, relevant, and hard-to-transfer knowledge and expertise possess the decision rights that enable the business to make use of what they know? If not, reallocate decision rights to those with the specific knowledge and information relevant to them. For instance, regional buyers who are intimately connected to customer tastes and preferences should have decision rights over the selection of seasonal models and fashion. And store managers who have knowledge of store-specific capacity constraints and displays should have specific decision rights over the selection of mixes of sizes and colors for each model.

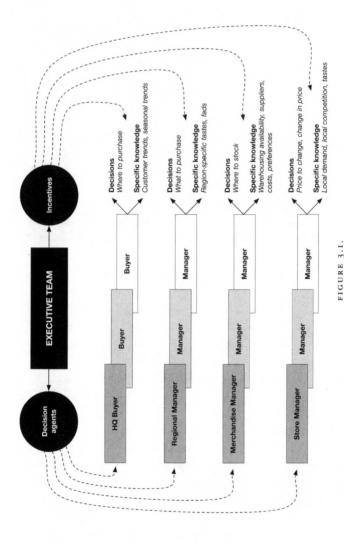

FIGURE 3.1.

The retailer's efficiency optimization challenge, defined as a problem of optimally allocating decision rights and incentives to managers at different levels of the organization, tasked with making different decisions within areas about which they possess hard-to-transfer knowledge.

"Wait a minute!" you might say. "How do we know which information, knowledge, and expertise is most useful, and who has them? After all, we need to know that the people we will give authority to are equipped to use it in the best possible way, which is knowledgeably."

Kinds of Knowledge and Ways of Knowing It: A Map

Good question. Knowledge and information are both tricky entities to "do things with" unless we have a good idea of how and why they make a difference in the business. Making good decisions requires knowledge and expertise—knowledge of both rules and of details; know-what, know-who, and know-how; and expertise in the process of making decisions. We need a map for figuring out which differences in knowledge or information make a difference and what difference they make. The decision agent flexon helps to unpack the diffuse and fuzzy entrails of knowledge and expertise into building blocks we can do something with. It helps us differentiate between different kinds of knowledge and information on the basis of how difficult it is to transfer from one agent to another.

Explicit knowledge is general knowledge of concept, theory, and general principle and knowledge of particular facts and data points—the stuff of everyday operational decisions and what we commonly call information. Some explicit knowledge is easy to transfer through vehicles like intranets, books, and the Web. In the case of our retailer, general accounting principles or general principles for optimizing the distribution and storage of the business are all easy to transfer. But quickly varying information, like local demand shortages, a frivolous new fad that has appeared in a region, or a local emergency that renders short the supply of parkas, is costly to transfer. It requires the rapid, reliable conveyance of information to the right person and at the right time.

Implicit knowledge is knowledge that is not articulated. It may be of an interpersonal nature—intimate know-who—relating to the tastes, preferences, quirks, and habits of particular people who trust a decision agent sufficiently to reveal themselves to her. It may be knowledge of some procedure—know-how—like walking or opening up the thorax with a scalpel, or relating to how to use the flexons to define, structure, and analyze business predicaments and synthesize solutions to the resulting problems.

We now have a map of knowledge. To organize it, we consider how costly knowledge is to transfer from one agent to another. At one end, specific knowledge is impossible or very costly to transfer and includes tacit know-how, intimate know-who, and quickly varying know-what. At the other end, general knowledge is easily and inexpensively transferable, like knowledge of principle, theory, and general fact. The principle of co-locating decision rights with knowledge that is hard and costly to transfer entails giving decision rights to those with decision-relevant specific knowledge. But, what, you may ask, is authority, that we may know what "transferring" it means?

Decision Rights: A Map of Authority

Decision rights are not all or nothing. They can be shared and distributed among many different people. From afar, however, decision rights look hard to divide: in plain language, it looks as if you either have authority or control over a decision, or you do not. This poses a significant challenge to using decision rights allocation to optimize the use of knowledge in a business: The decision agent flexon offers a way to split up decision rights by distinguishing among different kinds of authority. The flexon can be used to image business problems in the same way in which a biologist uses a scanning electron microscope to distinguish among different structures within a cell. We can distinguish among:

- *Initiation rights*: Who may start a decision process and articulate the set of alternative options?
- *Articulation rights*: Who may formulate what the options are?

- *Ratification rights*: Who may give final and binding approval for making a decision?

- *Implementation rights*: Who may implement the action plan corresponding to a decision that has been ratified?

- *Monitoring rights*: Who may monitor and measure the outcome of the implementation of a decision?

- *Sanctioning rights*: Who may assign differential rewards to agents on the basis of their performance?

- *Information rights*: Which agents may know what, and when? What may an agent expect to know, and when? Before the decision is made? After the decision has been made?

Now we can pose sharper questions regarding the allocation of decision rights among managers and employees within the retailer. For example, do store employees have specific knowledge that should be incorporated in the choice of styles and sizes? If they do, we can give them decision articulation and initiation rights without the ratification rights required to make the decision final. Do headquarters managers have unique information about suppliers' costs that will make them better negotiators? Then we can give them decision initiation rights over the timing and sequencing of purchase decisions, alongside decision ratification rights over the final choices of suppliers and quantities. Do regional managers have unique expertise in picking out the right styles for each region, according to each season? Then we can give them more decision articulation and joint ratification rights over the final product mix.

Efficiency—what we started out trying to improve—acquires a more precise meaning. It can be optimized by allocating decision rights to agents so as to minimize, first, the opportunity costs of forgone information and expertise. These are the often invisible costs the business incurs when decisions are made on the basis of less than all relevant information and expertise available among its managers and employees. Second, it can minimize the costs of coordination among various agents who have some kind of decision right. These are the costs of blow-ups, debacles, scandals, misunderstandings, and other failures of synchronization and commonality of meaning and purpose arising when agents are unclear about who can do what to whom. Finally, it can minimize the costs of communication among different people or groups with joint decision rights over a common set of decisions. If several managers who participate in making a decision have valuable and nonoverlapping knowledge and expertise (otherwise why give them all decision rights?), getting the relevant information to all of these people involves a process of explanation, messaging, answering, questioning, answering, and so on that can require a large number of steps.

Now we have a composite cost measure that we can use to gauge the consequences of reallocating decision rights. This allows us to devise both thought experiments and real experiments to figure out the best authority structure for our retailer. We can estimate and predict:

- The cost consequences of decentralizing decision ratification rights over apparel models and sizes to the level of the individual department store. Will coordination cost increases outweigh the decrease in opportunity costs? Will a new distributed information platform that allows all buyers access to the entire set of apparel models reduce these coordination costs?

- The cost consequences of decentralizing or centralizing decision initiation rights over suppliers or classes of suppliers. Will giving initiation rights over certain product lines to regional or store-level buyers increase coordination costs? Can a technological solution help?

- The effects of simultaneously decentralizing decision initiation rights and centralizing decision ratification and monitoring rights over apparel models, sizes, and colors. Will store- and regional-level buyers use their decision initiation and articulation rights if they do not have ratification or joint ratification rights?

. . . and so forth. The new language system has just unpacked the Pandora's box of the retailer's organization and made it possible to consider a set of changes that could produce significant enhancements in productivity.

For information and knowledge to function as value drivers, they need to be known—but also known to be known by others who are thereby on the same page (figure 3.2) We distinguish among different degrees of commonality in which knowledge and information are held. At one end of the spectrum, information may be private. A store manager may know of a quirk in the tastes of local buyers, but no one else within the organization does, so if she does not have the right to make purchasing decisions, that information is lost. At the other end of the spectrum, information is common knowledge: everyone knows it, everyone knows that everyone knows it, and so forth. If everyone from headquarters to the regional department store knows that the reliability of a key supplier has dropped off recently, then everyone can coordinate in making decisions about alternative sources of apparel.

We can also have in-between states of "knowing": a piece of information is known to everyone, although no one knows that others know it as well (a regime of distributed knowledge): collective action here will not be easy to coordinate. Or we can have a situation in which each agent knows that every other agent knows a bit of information, but not that every other agent knows that our agent knows that the other agent knows it (mutual knowledge). This regime can facilitate mobilization ("I'll go if you go"), but coordination ("I need to know you know I know where we are heading with this") may be harder. These distinctions let us figure out which pieces of information need to be mutual or common knowledge in order for managers and employees to coordinate their actions and where there are opportunities for interventions

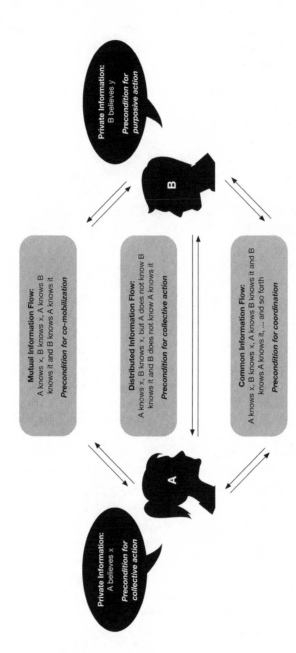

FIGURE 3.2.

Information and knowledge regimes, understood in terms of sharedness and commonality of a piece of information.

that pool information and create pockets of common knowledge to decrease coordination costs.

That gives us a map of information regimes within our retailer, so we can ask some more questions. First, what demand- and supply-side information needs to be common knowledge among managers within a department store or regional head office? We can use this information to create a commonly accessible database that pools it in order to facilitate dissemination and distribution at the regional level. Second, what demand- and supply-side information needs to be common knowledge among managers in the regional head office and in the headquarters office? We can use the answer to this question to create an internal repository of time-sensitive industry data that automatically pings all decision makers who have logged in and also shows everyone else the list of who has logged in and when, which will make the data not only widely known but also widely known to be known.

When we figure out what operational and organizational information needs to be common knowledge among executive team members, we can create mechanisms such as commonly agreed-on agendas, weekly senior management meetings and protocols for running them, and distributed information systems that comprise an effective dashboard that is known (and known by all to be known) to all of the executive team members.

Incentive Design and Alignment

There is a lot we can do to increase efficiency by just reallocating decision rights throughout a business. There is even more we can do if we also consider the motivations and incentives of key decision makers. Decision agents act in ways that maximize their own payoffs and interests and not necessarily those of the business. This gives rise to a set of agency costs when managers and employees take actions that are in their interests but not in the interests of the business. Examples are inefficient investment in corporate jets

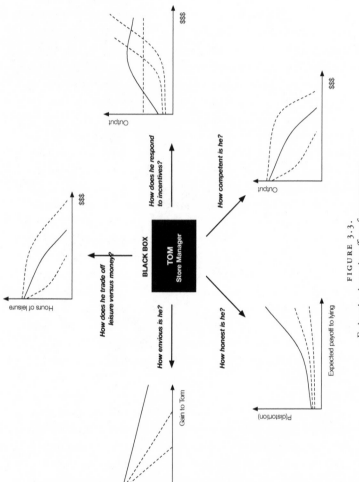

FIGURE 3.3.
Estimating incentive effects for a manager.

that enhance the status and prestige of the executives flying in them but are negative net present value projects for the business, or piling up sick days and then taking them all at once at the tail end of a vacation to put together a mini-sabbatical at precisely the most delicate time for the enterprise.

To understand the effects of different kinds of incentives on individuals, we need to understand the different objectives and interests of the agent whose behavior we are considering changing by changing its incentives. Will changing this agent's incentive structure motivate him or her to be more productive? This is not an easy question: people differ significantly in the way they respond to incentives. The flexon supplies a language for making sense of behavior patterns by estimating and measuring the effects of different kinds of incentives on a person.

Consider Tom, a department store manager. We can ask how he trades off leisure versus money. The answer will provide a sense of how much longer he is willing to work for contingent cash or stock compensation. The answer to the question of how much more intensely he will work for contingent financial compensation will give us a sense of how much harder he is willing to work for more money. Asking how his actual output or productivity will vary with greater levels of effort will give a sense of how competently he will work for more compensation. Asking how likely it is for him to distort (lie, fabricate, shade, color) information when he has an incentive to do so will give a sense of how reliable he is as a conveyor of useful information. And asking how he trades off gains to himself (monetary or otherwise) against losses to others on the same team will give us a sense of how envious he is and therefore how likely to destroy team output in order to increase personal welfare. Figure 3.3 maps out the possible results of turning answers to these questions into possible measurements. The flexon provides the palette to build a quick and accurate portrait of Tom in terms of the kinds of incentives he responds to as a result of the trade-offs apparent in his behavior.

With this portrait in hand, we can think of optimizing the incentive structure of Tom's contract. To do so, we distinguish two kinds of incentives with respect to their effects on his behavior. One is intrinsic incentives: To what extent is the agent motivated by the performance of an action as a good in itself? This is difficult to change, and modifying the incentives will usually require replacing the agent, making structural changes that enable him or her. The other kind is extrinsic incentives: To what extent is the agent motivated by an ulterior end or goal in performing an action?

Our levers for inducing behavioral change come in two different classes:

- *Financial incentives.* To what extent is the agent motivated to work for cash and equivalents (shares, warrants, options, no-recourse personal loans)? These are incentives we can change by modifying the fixed (contingent salary increases) or variable performance-based bonus, shares, options, and so on of the agent. They may include changes to the equity structure of a business (management buyouts) or changes to the debt-equity mix that finances the organization's projects (leverages recapitalizations).

- *Nonfinancial incentives.* To what extent is the agent motivated by nonfinancial incentives that are nonetheless externally provided? These include power (more decision rights over more decisions), professional and social status, and perquisites (remember the corporate jet). These are incentives we can modify by changing organizational context.

Aligning the Incentives of Agents with Those of the Organization

Once we understand the motivational structure of the agent by figuring out what payoffs could make a difference to behavior, we can use an alignment principle to tailor its incentive structure. For example, we can aim to mitigate the agency costs of Tom's employment relationship by offering him incentives that peak at exactly the points where the value to the retail chain of Tom's actions is maximal. For instance, we can make more of his annual cash compensation contingent on store-level efficiency measures (low inventory levels, high margins at the product level), which aligns his cash compensation incentive with the financial payoffs at the store level. A second possibility is to make his total compensation level contingent on store- and regional-level performance, which aligns his incentives with those of the regional office and disincents behavior that makes the store thrive at the expense of other stores in the region. A third option is to make part of his compensation dependent on 360-degree personal performance evaluations, which makes his incentives respond to changes in key indicators of store-level performance, like employee morale.

We can move the lens of the decision agent flexon upward to unpack and optimize the incentives of regional managers and merchandising managers in the headquarters store. Or we can move the lens downward to consider the incentives of managers within a single store. We can focus the lens of the flexon to adjust the incentives of individual managers according to what we know about the kinds of decisions they make and the ways in which incentives matter to the way they make them, or we can lump together managers of different ranks and design incentives that apply to the specific hierarchical rank.

Putting It Together

The fully developed semantics for organizational problem solving that we have assembled, the flexon in figure 3.4, features a set of basic entities we can use to make sense of the situation (decisions, agents, decision rights, knowledge, incentives) and a couple of optimization principles that allow us to generate solutions. First, a decision rights allocation principle tells us to assign rights over

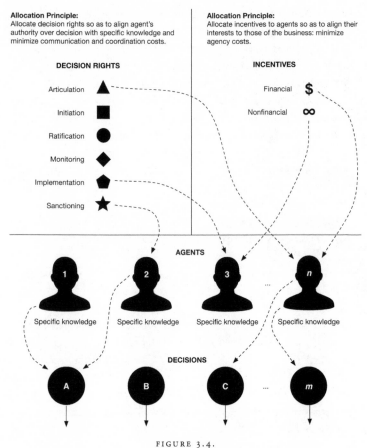

Allocation Principle:
Allocate decision rights so as to align agent's authority over decision with specific knowledge and minimize communication and coordination costs.

Allocation Principle:
Allocate incentives to agents so as to align their interests to those of the business: minimize agency costs.

FIGURE 3.4.
Using the decision agent flexon as an organizational design tool.

decisions to agents with the specific knowledge most valuable to making those decisions competently and in such a way as to minimize communication and coordination costs. Second, an allocation principle tells us to give the agents with the greatest level of decision authority incentives that will align their incentives with those of the organization. Now we can generate both alternative

ways of carving up authority (decision rights) and ways of divvy-
ing up payoffs (incentives) that are likely to lead to a better way
forward—in our terms, a solution.

THINKING THROUGH WHAT OTHERS WILL DECIDE
BEFORE DECIDING

The decision agent flexon is equally potent as a tool for thinking
through strategic interactions among agents. It lets us picture and
weigh the effects of agents' decisions on one another. Its use can save
us from many blind alleys that temporarily look like bright ideas.

Let's go back to 1987 for an example. North American car-
makers are reeling from the onslaught of Japanese car companies
like Datsun, Honda, Mazda, and Toyota that lure worldwide
customers with their innovative, sleeker, and more fuel-efficient
models. Both top-line revenues and net income are under assault
in Detroit's corporate headquarters. More worrying, market
share, held at the time to be a leading indicator of profitability, is
dwindling at General Motors, Ford, and Chrysler. At the same
time, fueled by worldwide expansion in airline travel, particularly in the business segment, the worldwide car rental business
is booming. Companies like Avis, Budget, Enterprise, and Hertz
have been joined in the expansion by newcomers like Budget,
Dollar, Thrifty, Snappy, and Alamo, which cater to different segments of the market. GM executives see an opportunity to lock
in demand for their new vehicles, smooth over revenue and earnings volatility, and increase market share in the bargain—if they
could lock one or more of the rental companies into buying
more of their models.

GM was first out of the gate when it acquired a 29 percent stake
in Avis for $135 million (in 1987 dollars) and proceeded to popu-
late Avis parking lots with new Chevys and Buicks. Ford immediately snapped up Hertz and Budget, and Chrysler soon after
bought Dollar and Thrifty. Each of the big three created a verti-

cally integrated value-linked buyer-seller network that locked large, steady buyers into their production line outputs of new models. This sounds like a textbook application of the decision agent flexon: create value by aligning buyer-seller incentives and taking away decision rights from pesky buyers whose tastes and budgets might steer them to Corollas and Camrys. Nine years later, each of the big three disgorged its prey: GM sold Avis back to a private equity group, as did Chrysler, and Ford gave up on its policy to force Hertz into buying its model cars. What happened?

The unpredicted but predictable choices of other participants in the market is what happened. Under the vertically integrated regime, car rental agencies took advantage of the influx of inexpensive late-model cars from their lead shareholders—the car companies—and became very large resellers of slightly used GM, Ford, and Chrysler vehicles in the second-hand car market. As a result, the resale value of Chevrolet, Buick, Ford, Lincoln, and other model cars plummeted by as much as 35 percent within three years from the date of the big three's acquisitions. In turn, that price drop sharply altered the incentives of another set of decision agents: the big three's new car customers. Conscious of the declining resale value of these models, they became even more price sensitive, which led to a further erosion in the top-line and bottom-line revenue and market share of the big three—a large delayed effect that could have been predicted had the executives who initiated the chain of transactions scoped out the entire car industry as a set of buyers and sellers making interdependent decisions.

We need to expand the canvas of the decision agent flexon to include the choices that this third set of agents can make as a result of the consolidation. In the case of the big three's debacle, the rental agencies had retained decision rights over selling their used cars at whatever time and price they chose so as to optimize their bottom line. And new car buyers' incentive to buy new Chevys would surely be affected by a lower expected resale value of their vehicle. We ask, What are their best responses to our moves? It may be that Ford would have been better off in a disintegrated industry. It may not have been optimal for it to buy Hertz had GM not bought Avis. But with one of the big three threatening to foreclose a very large segment of the buyer market, Ford's best response may well have been to respond in kind. The same logic applies to Chrysler. The best responses of new car buyers to the decrease in the resale price of new model vehicles would have been simple enough to predict from their earlier choices—when better Japanese models became available: go elsewhere!

What are our best responses to their best responses? The answer to this question would have turned up, "Go back to the status quo!" as an answer and saved everyone—not least the new buyers of brand-new Chevys, Tauruses, and Dodges—a lot of capital.

The decision agent flexon turns up a strategic simulation engine, which is best used not by thinking all the way to the Nash equilibrium wherein everyone makes an optimal choice conditional on everyone's else's choices being optimal as well, as some game theorists might advise. Rather, not everyone can or will want to think that far ahead, and the very idea of equilibrium requires that every agent know what every other agent knows about the situation at hand, including everyone's strategies, payoffs, and strategic options (And when, except in carefully constructed lab experiments, have you seen *that*?) We can, however, generate significant insight by using the decision agent flexon in a multiagent mode: construct careful models of the incentives, decision rights, information, and knowledge of each agent and then think through the reaction function of each agent to each of our feasible options:

- What is their feasible best response?
- What is our feasible best response to their feasible best response?

. . . and so forth. Each turn of the crank generates new perspectives on both what we could do and what they are likely to do, enabling greater insight into what we should do.

The leaders of a health service organization in a European capital city believed patients could be better served at a lower cost if care was more tightly integrated among primary, secondary, social, and mental health providers. But substantial barriers stood in the way of making integrated care a reality, from incompatible technology systems to the lack of a unified view of the services provided to any individual patient. The client seeks help in designing and implementing an integrated care pilot for patients in two priority groups: people with diabetes and the elderly.

Specify

Define the agents to focus on: the patients (people with diabetes and the elderly), the patient-facing staff (physicians and nurses), and secondary health care providers (technicians) and administrators.

We specify the key decisions made by each of the agents whose outcomes contribute to the performance of the system: whom to admit, where to admit (in-patient or outpatient), how long to admit for, which primary care services to contact, what to contract with them for (ongoing care versus short-term care), whom to discharge, when to discharge, what the long-term care protocol is. We can use scale (How many others does the decision affect?) and scope (What is the range of options the agent has?) to figure out which decisions are most worth zeroing in on.

We specify the decision rights (e.g., initiation—patient; ratification—admissions staff; ratification—primary health care provider) that the different agents may have and the possible incentives (such as lower wait times for patient), lower probability of readmission (hospital), and lower daily patient load (staff) that are operative for the different classes of agents.

We specify the decision: specific knowledge regarding the subjective condition of the patient (patients, admission staff), objective condition of the patient (primary care physicians), and underlying pathological processes (different health care practitioner specialists). We also specify a composite performance measure that incorporates short-run readmission and morbidity rates, patient satisfaction, hospitalization time, probability of readmission within one month of release of the patient, and even long-run morbidity and mortality outcomes, as well as a cost-reduction target (say, 20 percent) for the achievement of the requisite level of performance, as well as a solution ratification date (say, two months) and a performance improvement target date (say, one year).

Estimate

We estimate the likely distribution of decision rights in the service organization on the key decisions (e.g., admission criteria, engagement of multidisciplinary teams, nature of these teams), incentives (financial and nonfinancial), and specific knowledge that is operative for the key decision. From longitudinal studies and repositories of industry best practices, we also estimate the effects of various incentives and decision right allocations on the cost-constrained performance levels in health service organizations. Where data are incomplete or unavailable, we use the basic solution concept (increase the alignment of individual and organizational objectives to decrease agency costs and co-locate decision rights with incentives and expertise to maximize decision outcome efficiency) to make sensible extrapolations.

Measure

We drill down to measure the variables that make the most of the difference in the case of our client: actual wait times, morbidity and co-morbidity rates, patient satisfaction, decision rights on the high-impact decisions (e.g., admission criteria, choice of services contracted for at admission, discharge criteria), and the actual incentives that drive the decision right holder to make certain kinds of choices (e.g., long wait times may lead patients to avoid hospital visits, which may lead to decreased quality of care because underlying conditions are not treated in precritical stages and higher probability of emergency hospitalizations).

Predict

Based on our estimates of the likely effects of changes in decision rights and incentives to performance measures and our measurements of the key sets of decision rights and incentives of agents, we make predictions regarding the effects of feasible changes in decision right allocations and incentive changes on performance. What happens if you give patients more decision rights about the services they want to contract with? What about nurses? What happens if you transfer long-term care rights from the independent specialists to one primary care physician? What is an incentive-compatible organizational arrangement that allows this redistribution to be implemented?

Optimize

We evaluate the alternative allocations of decision rights and incentives to patients, physicians, and staff and choose the set that is most likely to (1) produce the performance improvement we seek within the time and cost constraints and (2) generate a plan we can elaborate within the time constraints of our engagement. We go back and forth between the predict and optimize steps as needed: we make predictions about what would happen if we gave patients more decision rights over specialist care options (say) and optimize when we evaluate the effects of the new decision right allocation on the performance of the system, discard inferior options and retain the superior ones.

This last step is in fact a double optimization: we are optimizing not only across possible solutions for the health service organization, but also across possible plans for searching for the optimal solution. The logic is simple: no solution, no matter how much better than the status quo it is, has an indefinite shelf life. The best-laid plans of today may be wasted on tomorrow. When we optimize, we do not simply solve problems like, "Find the fastest path from Park Avenue and 65th Street to LaGuardia Airport on a Friday afternoon at 2:15," but, "Find the fastest path to LaGuardia airport on a Friday afternoon by the fastest method for doing so." This is a double optimization problem. You first have to look for the fastest way of finding the fastest path (*Google* Maps? Yahoo Maps? Other maps? Some trusted cabbie? How do you know the fastest way of finding the fastest path? Your own experience? Others' experience? Statistical models?) before using that way to find the fastest route. One more case in which the logic of practice is markedly different from the logic of theoretical knowledge!

▶ YOU MIGHT WISH TO CONSIDER . . .

How would you apply the networks flexon to frame this last chal-lenge into a problem statement?

FOR FUN AND PRACTICE: MORE CHALLENGES

1. A European public health system struggled to determine why fewer than 10 percent of patients started, much less com-pleted, a diabetes disease management education program after receiving a diagnosis from their doctor. The public health impact of unmanaged diabetes is clear, yet the reasons patients were not participating in support programs were not. This population presented a challenging profile: many patients had low household incomes, and the prevalence of the disease in these subgroups resulted in higher-than-average complications and deaths. The client needs help identifying

the causes of poor program attendance and develop new approaches that can increase participation to an aggressive goal of 70 percent.

2. A leading bank with a commercial loan portfolio of more than $50 billion has seen charge-offs grow at a tenfold pace in 2013, and the lifetime charge-off has been estimated at 6 to 10 percent of the portfolio. The bank has asked for help with its workout capabilities, which have suffered from lack of clarity on process ownership, inefficient processes, widely dispersed data, misalignment of talent to deal needs, and limited risk-based prioritization.

3. Two companies in the food and beverages sector were entering a merger of equals prompted by shareholders who wanted to develop the business globally. The two companies had been fierce competitors and had very different cultures: one was hierarchical, the other entrepreneurial. The board members responsible for integration recognized that the clash of cultures would need to be managed carefully to minimize disruption and establish a constructive working environment. He asked for help to make the merger happen and prepare leaders for the integration process and their roles in the new organization.

IF YOU WANT MORE: ANNOTATED BIBLIOGRAPHY

For the nuts and bolts of the decision agent flexon—decisions, choices, utilities, beliefs and decision agents—see:

Kreps, D. (1988). *Notes on the Theory of Choice*. Boulder, CO: Westview Press.

Gilboa, I. (2011). *Rational Choice Theory*. Cambridge, MA: MIT Press.

Binmore, K. (2009). *Rational Decisions*. Princeton, NJ: Princeton University Press.

For an applied modeling approach that uses the decision agent flexon as a mapping, modeling, intervention, and behavioral modification tool for individual humans, see:

Moldoveanu, M. (2011). *Inside Man: The Discipline of Modeling Human Ways of Being*. Stanford, CA: Stanford University Press.

For an elaboration of decision rights and incentives and their use as modeling tools in organizations, see the collection of papers in:

Jensen, M. (2000). *Foundations of Organizational Strategy*. Cambridge, MA: Harvard University Press.

For foundational texts on game theory at an introductory level, see:

Osborne, M., and A. Rubinstein. (1994). *A Course on Game Theory*. Cambridge, MA: MIT Press.

For foundational texts on game theory at a more advanced level, see:

Fudenberg, D., and J. Tirole (1995). *Game Theory*. Cambridge: MIT Press.

For applied approaches to game theory, see:

Gintis, H. (1999). *Game Theory Evolving*. Princeton, NJ: Princeton University Press.

Kreps, D. (1990). *Game Theory and Economic Modeling*. Oxford: Oxford University Press.

4 THE SYSTEM DYNAMICS FLEXON

As the president of a $70 billion consumer goods company with an overwhelming share of many household brands markets and a mandate to reduce the rising costs of research, development, distribution, and marketing by as much as 15 percent, C. Exekoff Isser had gone through several rounds of overhead cost estimates, analyzed the effects of overhead cost cuts, studied the human resources cost structure and head count of each of the business's major divisions, and mandated analyses of the expected value of research and development activities across all of the firm's product lines. These analyses revealed a mostly lean organization. Cuts and reductions were likely to have an impact on its ability to deliver its next-generation products to market on time or sustain its current commitments for existing products. There was limited appetite inside the executive team to engage in a redesign of the firm's compensation system; a similar exercise two years before had produced no significant results in spite of the large cost of determining the optimal incentive structure for key employees and making changes in base pay and contingent compensation. The challenge he had been given by the board seemed intractable.

While pondering the difficulty, Isser remembered that one of his senior advisers had suggested he think of the business as one very large set of pipes and storage tanks through which product at different levels flowed to the distributors and end customers just like electricity across the grid of a major city. For a multi-billion-dollar annual revenue business selling on every continent, the smoothness of the product flow was crucial: unexpected delays in order fulfillment, sudden pile-ups of inventory—either internal or at the distribution centers—and uncertainty in the demand for various products on the shelves of the retail outlets had large cost consequences because inventory space had to be paid for and empty shelves meant business lost to competitors and potential foreclosure of the shelf space.

Following his intuition, Isser asked his operations team to design, build, and deploy a distributed information and communication system to smooth out the flow of products from conception, design, and prototyping through manufacturing to the end customer. The system was to provide real-time tracking measurements for each product, along with estimates of demand at the level of each store and region. Spikes in demand and supply would be singled out and addressed immediately by increasing or decreasing shipment flow rates, making precommitments aimed to safeguard shelf space, or liquidating inventory at prices that would allow the market to clear more quickly. The information system overlay, together with the small organization built to run it, ended up saving the business $700 million over six years, thus delivering on the mandate that Isser had received from his board.

What is special about the picture Isser used to think through his problem is that it focuses on the timing and sequence of events, both critically important in an operations-heavy business whose effectiveness depends on whether, when, and how reliably orders are fulfilled. This picture brings out the importance of timing by zeroing in on stockpiles and bottlenecks of product, materials, and money, which flow through a business the way water flows through the hydraulic system of an airplane and blood through the vessels of a mammal's body. The picture also focuses on the impediments and constraints to flow: limited shelf space, small warehouses for inventory, and seasonal limits to demand for a product in a region. A slow, unreliable distribution channel looks like an impedance. The end customer market looks like "a sink" for the products of the firm. Effects take time to propagate through the business. Seemingly small causes can have disproportionately large effects. Clearly it is important to have a problem-solving language that focuses the mind's eyes on delays and nonlinearities, which is what the system dynamics flexon does.

THE CAUSAL STRUCTURE OF A BEER DISTRIBUTION CHAIN

A well-known illustration of the flexon is a dynamical model of a supply chain called the beer game, shown in figure 4.1. It features a simple logistical system linking a beer factory to its consumers through two intermediaries: a wholesaler and a retailer. Orders flow from one stage to the next. They determine production levels, which drive shipment flows. The inventory levels act as buffers. Processing orders and delivering product takes time, so delays have to be introduced in the model. Causal relationships among variables in the system (orders→fulfillment, product testing→shipping, shipping→receiving) may be modeled as positive (+) or negative (–): an increase in one variable (the cause) will have a positive or negative effect on an increase in the other (the effect).

There can also be textured degrees of impact: the percent increase in daily production that an unexpected order of size Y will cause or the probability that an unexpected order of size Y will cause a increase in daily production of at least y units. Feedback loops can be introduced to account for the effects of a set of variables at one time on the value of other variables in the future: prior order count will figure into expectations of future order count, which will have an impact on current order fulfillment.

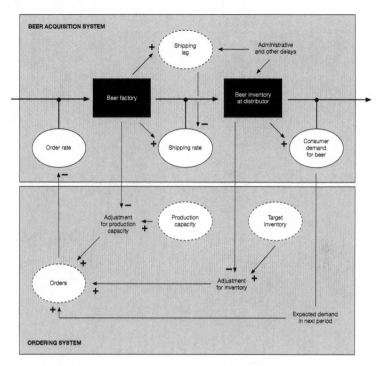

FIGURE 4.1.
A system dynamics map of the beer game.

Once we've built up this model, we can use our understanding of the beer maker's business to adjust its components for a desired response. We can systematically deal with the costs that accrue to the business because of delays, stochasticity, and nonlinearities: higher inventories (storage costs, cash flow uncertainty) and unfulfilled orders (opportunity costs, competitive costs). We can ask:

- *Where are the critical delays in the flow of beer to the user?* We can estimate the delays introduced by each stage of the distribution chain—manufacturing, storage, distribution, warehousing, transportation—and seek to decrease them by adjusting variables such as layout of the manufacturing location, shipping order sizes, and mixes of products.

- *Where are the critical delays in the flow of information from the outlet to the production line?* We model the flow of information about demand at the level of stores and regions in terms of the individual stages—from store-level estimates, to order processing, to product selection—and seek to minimize both the delays and the distortions in this information by introducing high-reliability tracking and forecasting systems that are common knowledge across the entire business.

- *What are the effects of nonlinearities such as batch order processing, manufacturing, packaging, and shipping on the size of the inventory and the probability of order fulfillment?* We can seek to reduce nonlinearities by diversifying the shipping and transportation network and implementing nimble, just-in-time manufacturing protocols that allow order batches to be filled by several different types of product that are going to different locations.

We have the rudiments of a new language system for thinking about business challenges—the *systems dynamics flexon*: *systems* because it looks at the business or industry as a whole as a set of stocks and flows of product and money and *dynamics* because we use it to figure out the response of the business to changes in stocks, flows, and their constraints. The system dynamics flexon lets us get precise about how quickly, how reliably, and how smoothly a business's operations change when key variables change so as to mitigate delays and adapt to stochasticity and nonlinearity.

Let's say we want to know what the effects are of investing an extra $10 million in marketing a new brand of toothpaste in a concentrated market. Looking at this through the system dynamics flexon lens, we can ask sharper questions—-for example, What are the time scales of the effects of an incremental investment in different channels, such as print media, social networking media, or broadcast media? This question can help us build a bottom-up answer to some more questions:

- How quickly can we expect to see demand increases in the product?
- How reliable is the effect of a marginal investment in each of these marketing levers?

These then give us a bottom-up approach to more questions:

- What is the probability of a demand increase given the increase in visibility for each medium?
- How large an increase in demand can we expect as a function of the increase in spending of marketing dollars? Is there a dollar threshold below which we see no effect or above which we see a disproportionately large effect or a diminishing one?

Like the other flexons, systems dynamics can operate at different levels of analysis:

- An overnight lending rate increase (the cause) can drive down the price of real estate in an area (the effect), which can cause an unexpected increase in the rate of bank foreclosures (a secondary effect), which can lead the central bank to hold off on further planned increases in the lending rate (the feedback effect).
- A sudden increase in the blood supply from donors can cause large and potentially damaging oscillations in the system storage reservoirs and processing centers that constitute the main inputs of a manufacturer of blood-plasma-derived products.
- A decrease in the blood glucose level of the CEO can cause a rise in his anxiety level at a board meeting, which will trigger an increase in the anxiety level of the whole team, which can cause the chief financial officer to distort critical financial information at the time of the next meeting.

We are inclined and often trained to think causally, so using the system dynamics flexon as a problem-solving language feels intuitive. However, the flexon also offers a route to being a lot more precise about effects that other flexons overlook: it takes causal thinking to its logical limit. To access this route, we need to overcome the feeling of comfortable familiarity and apply its logic as rigorously as that of any other flexon. To make system dynamic sense of a business challenge, we apply the same divide-and-conquer logic used before:

1. We parse the challenge into a set of dependent variables— what we are trying to predict or control and can measure (the outputs)—and a set of independent variables—what we believe will influence the set of dependent variables (the inputs).

2. We divide the independent variables we can measure into those we can control (levers) and those we cannot (exogenous variables).

3. We estimate the nature of the relationships between the independent and the dependent variables. To do this, we ask, Are they probabilistic or deterministic? Linear or nonlinear? Instantaneous or delayed?

4. We estimate probabilities, delays, and the functional form of the relationships between the independent and dependent variables.

5. We measure the current set of variables and predict which changes in the variables we can control are most likely to produce desirable changes within a specified period of time

6. We optimize by choosing the combination of changes in the variables we can influence that are most likely to produce the largest desirable change in the shortest, or the specified, period of time.

MAKING IT MORE PRECISE:

MODELING STOCKS AND FLOWS OF MATTER AND MONEY

To get a handle on this way of seeing the world, you need to take the same kind of view of a business that a control systems designer takes of a car's suspension system. It is a complicated piece of machinery, but it can be unpacked by considering what it is made of (its structure) and what it does (its function) . A change in momentum, for example, the car hitting a bump in the road, propagates as a force ($f(t)$) through the components of the system, which is designed to attenuate large-scale shocks and stop the car from bouncing up and down. Components like dashpots (d) absorb the momentum and dissipate the kinetic energy imparted by the car hitting the bump. Springs (s) store and then release energy. Their springiness and location within the suspension system determine the way in which the rider feels a bump. A force applied by a bump to the components in contact with the road— the tires and the wheels of the car—propagates upward through the suspension system in the same way that a surge in water flow propagates through the plumbing of a house.

The suspension system works if its response to bumps of various magnitudes matches the rider's expectations and preferences: more springiness for a sportier car and a smooth-as-silk suspension system for a luxury sedan. The basic idea of the mechanical model is that we can quantify and design subtle properties of the system ("smooth as silk") by the disciplined measurement of individual components (masses, springs, and dashpots; their inertia, viscosity, and elasticity) and the optimization of their topology, that is, the way they come together. By understanding the dynamical response of each component and of combinations of components, we can design suspension systems with overall responses that feel right, which thereby acquires a far more precise meaning.

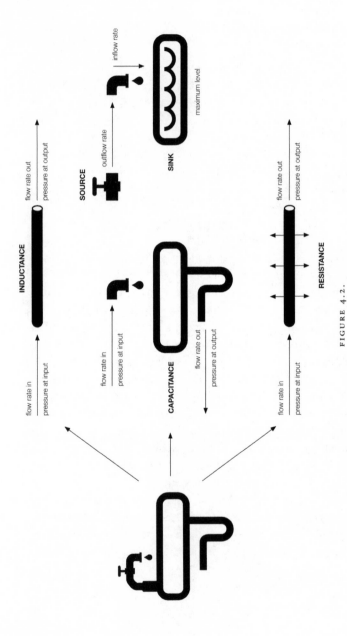

INDUCTANCE

flow rate out
pressure at output

flow rate in
pressure at input

SOURCE

outflow rate

inflow rate

SINK

maximum level

CAPACITANCE

flow rate in
pressure at input

flow rate out
pressure at output

RESISTANCE

flow rate out
pressure at output

flow rate in
pressure at input

FIGURE 4.2.

Expanded set of building blocks for describing a system in the language of the system dynamics flexon.

The propagation of a bump through components of the suspension system of the car provides a useful mental image of the propagation of causal influences like surges in inventory or free cash flows through a business. Each component of the suspension system responds to the force applied to it in a way that can be described by its reaction time constant and the amplitude of the causal influence that emerges from it. Analogously, a business can be broken into different components that act as sources, sinks, conduits, dissipators, and storage units for flows of matter and money. Their collective behavior can be understood bottom-up—a function of their individual behaviour and their relationships to one another.

To do this, we need a few more building blocks. Figure 4.2 shows these building blocks for a physical system, the most intuitive to grasp:

- We use flow variables to denote flows of matter (products or raw materials) and money (cash inflows and outflows).

- We use stock variables, such as pressure and inertia, to model quantities that drive changes in flow variables. Think of pressure differences between the in- and out-valves of a fluid flow line driving the flow rate of fluid through that line. Or consider the difference between supply and demand driving the flow rate or product (provided that we do not have the dreaded pile-ups and shortages) from the business into the market.

- We use a set of passive elements like inductors, capacitors, and resistances to model the relationship between the flow and stock variables in various components of the operations of a business.

We use the components of the system dynamics problem-solving language to get a better handle on business-relevant phenomena like these:

- *Losses*: We model lossy components of an operation (e.g., a manufacturing line in which some raw material is wasted or a transportation system in which a few shipments are lost) as resistors that dissipate the flow of matter or product through the operations.

- *Pile-ups*: We model pile-ups of products or matter or money by capacitances that accumulate flows of matter and money and then empty out in a way that can trigger reverberations and oscillations.

- *Bottlenecks and chokes*: We model bottlenecks within the business as inductors that capture systematic, structural delays in flows of matter and money.

- *Originators*: We model generators of inflow of matter and money through sources that produce a flow rate that the business as a whole must deal with.

- *End destinations*: We model the target destination of the flows of matter, money, and product, such as a paying customer base, as sinks that have some maximum absorption capacity (a saturated market) for the incoming flow (product at a given price).

CHALLENGE

Our business is a multibillion-dollar-revenue blood plasma products and derivatives manufacturer facing the challenge of sudden volatility in the blood plasma products and derivatives market and declining operating margins on its blood harvesting (from donors), refinement, distribution, and delivery operations. Its executive team is struggling with the difficulty of getting a grasp of the situation and is asking for help in formulating a strategic and tactical plan over two years.

Enter the system dynamics flexon. We specify the problem by following the plasma flow through the operations of the business, shown in figure 4.3.

- We map the sources of plasma—donors and collection centers—as a source coupled to a capacitance with fast decay times (unprocessed plasma has a short shelf life).

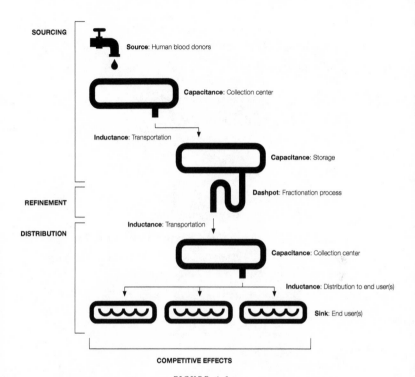

FIGURE 4.3.
A specification of the challenge in the language of the system dynamics flexon.

- We use resistances to denote the loss of plasma in processing and distribution.

- We model plasma distribution systems through inductances that throttle down the maximum flow rate of plasma and derivatives on account of capacity constraints, and net efficiency losses (or yield reductions) in the plasma processing plants through resistances.

- We model the demand for blood plasma and blood plasma products using a sink (or a collection of coupled sinks) whose capacity is determined by the total addressable market and competitive effects. We then model the distribution systems (via hospitals and infusion centers that are responsive to alternative sources and to alternative therapies) by inductances whose net impedance varies in proportion to the net inflow of relevant alternatives into the market and the demand for the different plasma fractions.

- We specify a set of levers associated with changes we can make in capacity (capacitors and inductors) and changes in the flow rate of plasma into collection centers (with more centers and more donors per center).

We estimate the relevant relationships of interest from available comparable data for the client and the industry:

- The average and maximum efficiency of the plasma fractionation processes (resistances), distribution systems (inductances), and storage systems (capacitances)

- The average and maximum plasma flow rates from the sources (donors in collection centers)

- The average and maximum achievable values of the sink capacities (total addressable market as a function of time) and changes in the impedance (losses and delays) of the system to changes in market share and to competitive entry and exit

We model the top-line performance of the business in terms of available demand at time T that can be uniquely fulfilled at time $T + t$ by a realistic capacity expansion (e.g., the decrease in impedance $\rightarrow$ increase in yield of plasma transformation) and bottom-line performance as an inverse of the total impedance of the system (measuring operational costs and the capital expenditures of capacity expansions).

We then zero in on and measure the donor plasma intake, the capacity of the storage system, the flow-through rate for the processing plants, and the delays and losses of the distribution system. We measure these quantities for relevant periods (a quarter, a year, five years) and calibrate the model to the actual business we are dealing with.

We can now make predictions about the efficiency of the system given the most likely scenarios of demand and supply expansion and contraction as a function of different capacity expansion and contraction choices that we have. We can zero in on doomsday scenarios (significant supply chain disruptions, the market flooded with alternatives) and halcyon scenarios (market demand expands, plasma fractionation yields increase) and model not only the absolute response of the system but also the transient response: meeting unexpected levels of demand at period $T + 1$ depends sensitively on having optimized the operation for a higher level of output at time T. We can not only shed light on whether to expand capacity now in order to meet an unexpected rise in demand but also where to make the key investment in expansion.

We optimize the operation of the business by selecting the combination of capacity expansion or contraction options (decrease inductance, decrease resistance, increase capacitance, increase mass flow rate) most likely to improve performance over the time frames we started with. We may find that increasing capacity is the (counterintuitive, given recent volatility) best option in uncertainty-weighted net expected value terms. In addition, we may also find that ownership of plasma collection centers is critical to a fast and effective response system to variations in market demand. Or we may decide to relocate some storage facilities for greatest average efficiency gain of the operation as a whole.

▶ YOU MIGHT WISH TO CONSIDER . . .

How would you use the decision agent flexon to transform this challenge into a well-defined problem? What about the networks flexon?

Using the system dynamics flexon, define and structure the following challenges:

1. A regional health system in Europe was having difficulty discharging elderly hospital patients in a timely fashion. The system knew that these patients were especially likely to need follow-up services from community health and social care providers—services that could be difficult to arrange. However, it also knew that delayed discharges jeopardized patients' health and increased costs unnecessarily. The system therefore thought that closer integration of acute care, community health, and social care services could accelerate the discharge process. However, it was uncertain about how big a problem it actually had, whether integrated care was the right solution, and whether other steps were needed to make the discharge process more efficient.

2. A large US regional bank, with more than $100 billion in assets and a significant retail presence with more than 1000 branches had consistent earnings with an above-average cost structure and flat revenue growth. A stable overall branch presence over three years had limited growth in rapidly growing areas. It asks for help to develop a comprehensive network optimization plan designed to enhance near-term profitability.

3. In July 2009, the European Union (EU) and Group of 8 announced an objective to reduce greenhouse gas emissions by at least 80 percent from the 1990 level by 2050 to combat climate change. What kind of transformation would this involve? How could the EU reconcile its environmental commitments with its aspirations for economic development and energy security? To support the EU's goal, a foundation launched a project to establish a fact base and explore the

implications of decarbonization for European industry and the power sector in particular. The EU asked for help to develop a set of ambitious yet feasible pathways for achieving a low-carbon economy.

Define and structure the challenges using another one of the flexons introduced earlier.

IF YOU WANT MORE: ANNOTATED BIBLIOGRAPHY

For a comprehensive approach to modeling causal systems that feature both deterministic and nondeterministic relationships, see:

Pearl, J. (2000). *Causality*. Cambridge: Cambridge University Press.

For a state-space approach to the modeling and analysis of dynamical systems, see:

Luenberger, D. (1993). *Introduction to Dynamic Systems: Theory, Models and Applications*. New York: Wiley.

For a detailed approach to the use of system dynamics modeling and mechanical and electrical systems using the generalized discipline of bond graphs, see:

Karnopp, D., D. Margolis, and R. C. Rosenberg. (2006). *System Dynamics: Modeling and Simulation of Mechatronic Systems*. New York: Wiley.

For an optimal control approach to modeling and simulation of macroeconomic systems, see:

Hansen, L. P., and T. S. Sargent. (2008). *Robustness*. Princeton, NJ: Princeton University Press.

Mag E. Director, the chief investment officer of private equity fund PEF with about $10 billion under management focused on leveraged, management-led buyouts of scalable midmarket firms valued in the range of $200 million to $2 billion, faced a sudden two-quarter drop in investment prospects and an increase in the size of the fund. The latter was driven by its incentive structure: a 2 percent fee for money under management and a 20 percent cut of returns over a 7 percent hurdle motivated the partners to raise bigger funds while keeping head count constant. The pipeline of deals coming before the investment committee tapered to a trickle during the last six-month interval in spite of the fact that the fund's popularity and prestige in the industries it targeted was un-diminished. When Mag looked carefully at the inflow of pros-pects, she found that the fund was not undersolicited by the standards of either historical deal inflow rates or the standards of other funds with the same size sand profile. Deals *were* coming. Investment-grade deals were not. What to do?

The incentive structure and decision right allocation of the fund had been tuned to motivate optimal investment decisions and intensive management-level involvement of the partners in the investee companies. The fund's performance showed improvement after the compensation plan had been finely tuned with the help of a major advisory firm. Against the advice of her investment committee, who was insisting that the fund's partners were not properly motivated to go out and get deals, Mag focused on the process by which investments were selected along the flow of the deal pipeline, including the initial filtering process, the due diligence process, the pruning process, and the final investment decision process. She found that early-stage decisions were made so quickly and decisively that there were only a very few investment prospects still in the running by the time due diligence was initiated. In turn, due diligence was done with great accuracy and precision, but with the clear intent to pass on rather than invest in the deal on the table. As a result, the investment committee was ending up with very few candidate companies in the running, many of which had already taken, with multiple term sheets pending, which decreased PEF's bargaining power.

Mag asked for a study of optimal selection processes for high-uncertainty prospects based on principles of natural selection and evolutionary programming, with a view to redesigning the processes by which her fund makes investment decisions. The completed study showed that given the hazard rates and volatility in the industries that her fund targeted and the number of target companies that came into the deal flow of the fund, a selection process that made a quick series of soft decision (decisions that could be reversed on consideration and due diligence) and a number of low-sunk-cost, low-cost-basis investments that would allow the fund to gather more information about a company from an insider perspective, would significantly outperform the current process. In that process, losers were irreversibly discarded early on, and the winners were the small group left standing. The insight led her to a redesign of the fund's selection process that significantly increased both the pipeline of investments going to the investment committee for final approval and the quality of the investments before the committee, compared with historical data. It turned up many hidden gems that would have been discarded by the old process, even after one round of implementation.

BUILDING UP THE EVOLUTIONARY FLEXON

The evolutionary flexon embodies the logic of natural selection. It sees businesses, teams, groups, and people as organisms that compete to survive in an ecosystem. The survival of each unit depends on its fitness level, which depends on the fit between its characteristics and the environment. The fittest survive, and the least fit perish. In the case of our private equity fund, the competing entities are the firms vying for capital. They are the population from which individuals are selected. The fund acts as a selection filter: the better the filter, the better the firms it selects do, and the better the fund does. Mag's reframing of the problem from one of getting the incentives of the partners right to one of getting the process of selection right was an evolutionary reframing of a problem usually tackled by optimizing incentives.

The evolutionary flexon does not just say, "Focus on selection processes and redesign them for optimal performance." Just as there is a lot more to evolution than selection, there is a lot more to the evolutionary flexon than just selection process design. Variation also counts: designing optimal businesses from scratch is often a fool's errand because the bases of advantage change frequently and unpredictably.

Seen as natural selectors, markets provide a shortcut to the design problem: they select the best among many ready-made businesses and let the others perish. A private equity fund provides a critical piece of this selection function by giving some businesses access to capital. It is in the selection business, the insight Mag used. But because the future sources of advantage in any market are difficult to predict, diversity and variety help. That is the role of random mutation in natural selection processes. In the private equity business, variation comes in the form of the spread of technologies, products, management approaches, and scale and scope of production functions of the businesses that go into the deal funnel. To get good deals into the pipeline, you need lots of different deals to come your way. There are lots of "cats and dogs" in the market looking for capital, which means that for every good deal there is, there are many poor ones. Your pool of firms seeking capital has to be deep. Dense populations of organisms mutate quickly to make substantial progress quickly, which is why we need a deep, dense pool of firms entering the prospect funnel.

Selection is not binary: it comes in many forms. Some are harsh and irreversible, others soft and reversible once more information becomes available. Some are fast, others slow. A chance mutation in a gene that codes for fur color can produce white foxes from red foxes, which, in an Arctic landscape, have a much better chance of bearing white, and therefore better-camouflaged, offspring. They are more likely to survive predators while they are too young to defend themselves and thereby further the lineage of white foxes. That, however, is a process that takes lots of time, something Mag rarely has lots of.

Software engineers have learned to design evolutionary algorithms that allow for selection rules that are both fast and soft. On the basis of rules of thumb, they select not just one individual (the fittest) but several (the 100 fittest) and do so quickly. They rank them and allow all of them to hang around for a generation or so just in case the selection rule was faulty or the environment changed. These are all useful principles for Mag: choose quickly, use clever decision rules, and make choices reversible. In addition, keep a number of prospects around because you never know where the next star will come from, and be ready to revisit the selection rules used along the way in case the business environment changes abruptly.

Through an evolutionary lens, a product design cycle looks like a massive variation-selection-retention process that we can improve once we map its evolutionary mechanics. The flexon lets us design the process by which we design things—for example, what tablet features will compete successfully with the latest iPad? No amount of predictive thinking, optimizing, and analyzing is likely to solve the problem by picking out the golden tablet. But an evolutionary approach to crafting small-scale experiments in the lab and the field could be highly effective, provided that we design the selection filters for promising solutions to mirror as closely as possible the selection filters that the product market will apply to the product. Alpha tests, beta tests, and engineering reviews can be designed to mimic as closely as possible the selection properties of the product market. It also yields a set of metrics by which we can track how well we do in this process: How harsh? How fast? How deterministic? How irreversible? These metrics allow us to ask sharp, pointed, and meaningful questions when we design lab and field tests.

Or: What collection of features and attributes should the next brand of toothpaste from a major manufacturer embody? We want something that outdoes its most popular brand without cannibalizing the different subbrands of that product. Painstakingly modeling the utility that different customer groups derive from different features and figuring out the globally optimal set of features for the new product is a huge undertaking in terms of data collection, the calculations required to figure out what the data say, and interpretation of that information. But by using an evolutionary lens, we can design the small set of maximally useful experiments, small and large, that will allow us to zero in on a better product.

As with the other flexons, we can apply the evolutionary flexon to view challenges at multiple levels of analysis, ranging from an individual to a whole industry ecosystem as shown in figure 5.1. A group (level 2) is a population of individuals (level 1), some of whom are selected for and some against according to a selection mechanism that may favor personality type, level of computational or social intelligence, conscientiousness, and so forth. In turn, an organization (level 3) is a population of groups that are themselves in competition for survival—the resource allocation process. They may be selected for on the basis of cohesion, the costs of coordination, levels of output (Is the whole greater than the sum of the parts?), and timeliness in the delivery of output. An industry (level 4) is an ecology of businesses. The product market (what customers choose to spend money on), the capital markets (what stocks investors buy), and the market for corporate control (what firms talented executives choose to work for) supply the selection mechanisms.

The discipline of using the evolutionary flexon as a problem-solving language is based on mapping the entities of our predicament into the variables of its language system. First, what are the entities and groups of entities on which mutation and selection operate? These are the analogues of organisms and populations in an evolutionary model. They may be people in a group, firms in an industry, individual products that are close substitutes in a competitive market, product features appealing to different tastes and preferences of the consumers, and so on.

We need to be precise about the analogues of genotypes and phenotypes. In an evolutionary model, a set of individual properties, the *genotype*, determines a set of individual characteristics, the *phenotype*, which shapes fitness. Individual entities usually cannot change their genotypes, and thus their phenotypes, quickly enough to adjust to the selection process. So the way to shape an evolutionary

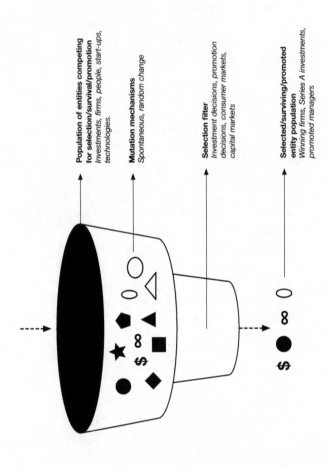

Population of entities competing for selection/survival/promotion
Investments, firms, people, start-ups, technologies.

Mutation mechanisms
Spontaneous, random change

Selection filter
Investment decisions, promotion decisions, consumer markets, capital markets

Selected/surviving/promoted entity population
Winning firms, Series A investments, promoted managers

FIGURE 5.1.
Schematic view of the modeling language of the evolutionary flexon.

process is to tinker with its variation and selection mechanisms. For instance, if the individual salespeople in a consumer goods business have stable (genotype) personality characteristics that cluster around Myers-Briggs variables (Introversion-Extraversion in attitude, Sensing-Intuition and Thinking-Feeling in functions, and Judging-Perceiving in orientation) and if their personality types drive their ways of being to clients, which in turn drives their ability to close sales and drive volume, then we can think of a client's sales force as a population ecology of people whose "genomes" are their personality traits, of which there are sixteen possible combinations. Their phenotypes are behavioral patterns associated with the various personality profiles. Their fitness function is their sales performance averaged over quarters or years.

▶ YOU MIGHT WISH TO CONSIDER . . .

To grasp the mechanics of the evolutionary flexon, create at least five different plausible ecosystems from your own experience, including evolving entities vying for survival, their genotypes and phenotypes, and specify the process by which they compete—the selection rules or performance measures (or both) and the ways in which their fitness is evaluated.

·   ·   ·

In an evolutionary picture of a business, randomness, usually considered the enemy, can be useful because it generates novelty. The evolutionary flexon encourages us to master the process of disciplined guessing. To do so, we need to be precise about the mechanisms that produce variation in the population of entities under consideration: the mechanisms of mutation, which come from noise and heterogeneity. We can introduce noise to induce mutations in a product design process by making small, random changes in feature sets—think of the many distinct features that can be changed ever so slightly in putting together a next-generation mobile tablet. We can also use heterogeneity to introduce variation in a population that is not as susceptible to random mutation: our PEF fund can broaden its net to include businesses in different industries, or in different components of the same industry, or make use of different techniques to solve the same problem.

When we tinker with processes, we need to be mindful of time, or the speed with which a process unfolds. The rate at which we produce variation is critical: mutate too quickly, and you do not have stable entities to select among; mutate too slowly, and you do not have sufficient variation to generate better entities in time to select from them. "Too quickly" is always defined relative to the rate at which we select. If the selection process works on scales of decades or centuries, as it does in the population of universities, then a mutation time constant of years may be just fine. If it works at the level of two to five years, as it does in closed-end private equity and venture capital funds, then a mutation time constant of weeks may be required.

Recombination through sexual reproduction affords the added degree of freedom of recombining the genetic material of the parents via sex, which mixes and matches the parents' genes s in the genotype of the daughter entities. A new toothpaste may have a large number of features, many of which come from several different parent toothpaste products (e.g., whitening, cavity protection) and have been recombined in the development process. A private equity firm may mix and match ideas, technologies, modules, and even management teams of the start-up and mature businesses it is considering or has already invested in.

Perhaps the key component of the evolutionary flexon is selection: How discriminating is the selection filter? Are all individuals who do not fulfill certain criteria discarded? Or are some of them given second and third chances, with diminishing probabilities of selection in subsequent rounds? Is the process geared toward selecting the best candidates or toward eliminating the worst? Does the process act globally (on the entire population) or locally (on pockets or niches of the population)?

To describe various selection mechanisms, we need a more precise language to capture the features of interest of an evolutionary process. Here are some useful candidates:

- *Ranking selection*, which sorts the population from best to worst and picks out the leaders according to their rank score. Ranking selectors can be linear or nonlinear, and they may be more or less severe. For instance, a pruning selection mechanism can be used to eliminate the worst k individuals from taking part in any further iteration of the variation-selection-retention process.

- *Tournament selection*, which picks k subsets of n candidates (64 subsets of 2 in the usual tournament format, like the US Open Tennis Championships). It picks the best of the subset and then discards the rest.

- *Proportional selection*, which evaluates individuals in the population according to their overall fitness. It then allows each to reproduce further such that the probability that any individual will reproduce rises monotonically with this performance measure.

▶ YOU MIGHT WISH TO CONSIDER . . .

Specify some of the selection processes you have been through as an individual person. Write down their characteristics in terms of reversibility, determinism, harshness, and rate.

PERFORMANCE MEASURES FOR SELECTORS

Selection mechanisms give us levers by which we play with the speed of a process. Different selection processes work at different speeds. It turns out that we can estimate the speed of a selection process by computing its time complexity—the number of operations required for the selection process to converge to an optimum as a function of the size of the population. How quickly can you winnow down a set of 1 million alternative product designs to just 1? We find that tournament ranking wins the speed race because it generates an optimum in a number of operations that is of the order of N, the number of individuals in the population. By contrast, a ranking-based process generates the optimum in $N \ln N$ operations, whereas a proportional selection mechanism generates it in a number of operations of the order of N^2. Evolutionary processes are distinguished by their speed of convergence, which means we can design the mechanisms of selection in ways that maximize this speed by lowering the requisite number of operations.

When selecting among selectors, we must balance speed against quality. Haste can make waste—but not always. One proxy for the quality of a selection process is the preservation of diversity of candidates—the basis for the advantage of evolutionary algorithms over other problem-solving procedures. Yes, a tournament is fast, and this is perhaps one of the reasons that promotion-based incentive schemes in hierarchies are so prevalent. But if, to go back to the tennis analogy, Roger Federer beats Mikhail Youzhny in the quarter finals and Murray beats Tsonga, then we will never know whether Federer would have beaten Jo-Wilfried Tsonga or Andy Murray would have beaten Youzhny. We do not, in other words, have a true ranking of the various options with respect to the quality of their features. All we have is a methodical elimination of options that are locally dominated. There is a diversity loss associated with the selection mechanism—the price we pay for speed, which we get by making selection irreversible—and it varies inversely with the speed of the selection process. Proportional selection gets us diversity at the expense of speed: fitness level affects the probability that an entity will be selected, which increases the range of entities that succeed. Therefore, it is possible, even if unlikely, that an inferior entity, which would have been squarely eliminated in a tournament, will still be allowed to survive in a proportional selection mechanism.

With these levers in hand, the basic scheme for solving problems using the evolutionary flexon becomes simple to understand: optimize the process at hand to produce the best offspring, or offspring-of-offspring, in the time allotted. The logic of mutation-variation-selection provides a set of tools for getting a grip on a large number of processes, ranging from investment selection to product design to the design of better-performing teams and groups. This grip comes in the form of a set of process variables—diversity, speed, and the nature of the selection process—by which we can selectively intervene in the relevant part of the business.

▶ YOU MIGHT WISH TO CONSIDER . . .

With the levers above in hand, redesign a selection process that you have personally been through for better results for the selector (not for yourself). Be sure to specify the selector's objective function and the relationship to the fitness function of the entities it is selecting for.

CHALLENGE

A North American state university system with a student enrollment of more than 1 million undergraduate and graduate students in state colleges and universities is under increasing pressure because of the simultaneous escalation of average costs (tenured faculty members and overhead) and declining willingness of new students to pay, driven by decreasing prospects of postgraduation employment. The system's chancellor is seeking new ways of addressing the skills gap that has emerged between graduating students and employers' expectations, including the complete overhaul of the system's recruitment, admissions and placement functions, as well as pedagogy and grading policy.

Seen through the evolutionary flexon's lens, a system of higher education is a massive selection engine. It selects students using admissions filters and selects the best students through grade distributions, thereby attracting recruiters who would like access to many students concentrated in one place and accurate information about the skills of graduates. We specify the population (individual students) and the selection filters (admissions processes and grades). We then specify the features of students as the skills, capabilities, and traits, including personality traits, that will make them maximally desirable in the labor market. These will include both cognitive and noncognitive skills, including self-command, self-control, empathic accuracy, and openness. We specify the degree of variation in the pool of applicants, the pool of admitted students, and the pool of top performers as the degree of variation in the characteristics that matter most to employers. Finally, we specify the speed of the selection process as the inverse of the period of time in which the system needs to provide recruiters information about individual students, ranging from a quarter to the duration of a program. We are now in the possession of a basic selection model for higher education that is highly parsimonious. We can seek to make significant improvements to the system without tinkering with variables like overhead cost, faculty pay, and faculty tenure, and teaching style and mode that are beyond the control of the administration.

We are poised to look at the challenge as a much tighter problem that relates to the optimization of a large-scale process of variation selection of students and graduates, based on a fitness function that measures the value of their skills and attributes to recruiters. We can estimate the correlation between the repertoire of skills and attributes of a graduate or a student and the value of that individual to the labor market. We can then create a composite measure of "fitness" for each individual that will shape the selection filters we design. We can use these high-level estimates and the set of variables we are focused on to measure the specific characteristics of students that recruiters who select candidates from the graduates of the university system focus on and the specific parameters of the evolutionary process embodied in them—for instance:

- The speed at which information about the value-added characteristics of a student or graduate becomes available to the university, the student, and recruiters

- The degree of variation in the value-relevant characteristics of students and graduates that is available within the applicant pool and the student body

- The recruiter-specific demand for students possessing certain subsets of characteristics and skills, as evidenced by past hiring decisions

These measurements, along with the basic principle of optimizing the selection process by changing the variability and number of competing individuals, the selection criteria and the selectivity of the selection filters (admissions, grading), and the speed with which selection filters, produce accurate and relevant information about value-relevant characteristics (measured monthly? quarterly? yearly?) to make predictions about the impact of different changes we could make to the university system. We can, for instance, ask, and answer, questions like these:

- What will be the impact on employability of redesigning admissions and standards processes to select for emotional and relational skills that are not captured by standard tests?

- What will be the impact on employability of redesigning evaluation systems to broaden the distribution of grades in order to allow students to differentiate themselves on relevant dimensions?

- What will be the impact on the employability of graduates of speeding up the process by which students receive detailed, specialized report cards on their performance on a set of measures of characteristics relevant to employers?

The answers allow us to optimize the university system's variation- and selection-related processes without requiring massive, uncertain, and costly global redesigns of its curriculum, pedagogy, and faculty compensation policies. We can seek to improve the filtering properties of the university system in these ways:

- Designing and implementing multidimensional measures of applicant qualities and characteristics that are in demand with leading recruiters and implementing selection mechanisms that use them

- Designing and implementing grading and evaluation systems that maximize the amount of information regarding the qualities and characteristics of students and maximize employers' ability to tell students apart

- Designing and implementing communication and marketing strategies aimed at attracting a maximally diverse group of applicants and enrolled students to the university system

▶ YOU MIGHT WISH TO CONSIDER . . .

How would you use the decision agent flexon to define and structure this challenge? What about the networks flexon? What about the system dynamics flexon?

FOR FUN AND PRACTICE: MORE CHALLENGES

Use the evolutionary flexon to define and structure the following challenges:

1. A regional health system in Europe was having difficulty discharging elderly hospital patients in a timely fashion. The system knew that these patients were especially likely to

need follow-up services from community health and social care providers—services that could be difficult to arrange. However, it also knew that delayed discharges jeopardized patients' health and increased costs unnecessarily. The system therefore thought that closer integration of acute care, community health, and social care services could accelerate the discharge process. However, it was uncertain about how big a problem it actually had, whether integrated care was the right solution, and whether there were other steps needed to make the discharge process more efficient.

2. A leading nonfood retailer was spending 15 percent of its revenues on market communication, especially on classic advertising. Executives at the company are uncertain about the value they were getting from the marketing outlay and need help to evaluate the size of the company's total marketing budget, how spending is allocated to different media, and how marketing efforts are influencing the consumer-purchase funnel.

3. The governor of Brazil's third largest state, Minas Gerais, committed to a bold vision: by the age of eight, every child would be reading and writing. That aspiration was particularly ambitious given the school system's 15,000 teachers for 130,000 students and low starting point (49 percent of eight-year-olds were reading at grade level). Nearly 3,000 individual schools would be involved, and many would need to make huge leaps of improvement from year to year. The government is asking for assistance in identifying the most promising measures that would bring about the desired change within four years.

Now go back and redefine and structure each challenge using one of the other flexons introduced earlier.

IF YOU WANT MORE: ANNOTATED BIBLIOGRAPHY

For a nontrivial account of evolutionary theory as a way of understanding the dynamics of life on earth, see:

> Gould, S. J. (2000). *The Structure of Evolutionary Theory*. Cambridge, MA: Harvard University Press.

For an application of evolutionary logic to the life and death of firms, see:

> Nelson, R., and S. G. Winter (1982). *An Evolutionary Approach to Economic Behavior*. Cambridge, MA: Harvard University Press.

For a methodical investigation of evolutionary algorithms as simulations of evolutionary processes of variation, selection, and retention, see:

> Back, T. (1996). *Evolutionary Algorithms in Theory and Practice*. New York: Oxford University Press.

For a more applied view of evolutionary algorithms, see:

> Goldberg, D. (1989). *Genetic Algorithms in Search, Optimization and Machine Learning*. Reading, MA: Addison-Wesley.

For a sociological perspective on markets as population ecologies of firms, see:

> Hannan, M. T., and J. Freeman. (1989). *Organizational Ecology*. Cambridge, MA: Harvard University Press.

For a mathematically precise treatment of evolutionary dynamics in genetically linked populations, see:

> Nowak, M. A. (2006). *Evolutionary Dynamics: Exploring the Equations of Life*. Cambridge, MA: Harvard University Press.

For a game-theoretic treatment of interactions and interdependencies in genetically linked populations, see:

> Weibull, J. W. (1995). *Evolutionary Game Theory*. Cambridge, MA: MIT Press.

6 THE INFORMATION PROCESSING FLEXON

Sergey Brin and Larry Page faced a challenge that may be para-phrased as follows: order the 1 billion web pages active in 1999 in a way that allows a user to effectively search these pages using simple queries, such as typing a word or a phrase into the text box of a search app. A successful search would return to the user an ordering of the pages containing a keyword or phrase, ranked ac-cording to its importance among all the other pages. To get a sense of the magnitude of the challenge, think of the World Wide Web as a network with 1 billion randomly connected nodes—the pages. The links between the nodes represent which page refer-ences which other page. Page-page links are citations that go from one page to another.

The challenge may trigger thoughts of the networks flexon: you can measure various network centralities of each page and dis-cover how many pages cite it, how likely it is that you have to pass through them to get from any page to any other page following citation paths, and how central the top 10 percent of the pages are that cite it.

It seems that all you need is to compute daily centrality mea-sures for the 1 billion web pages. Then list them, rank them, and presto! you have your solution. Unfortunately, the procedures for calculating centrality take a LOT of time to implement, and they are laborious. To calculate the betweenness centrality of 1 billion pages, you may need up to a billion billion billion billion operations. That means you could not get it done in one day on existing (1999) hardware. Remember: taking more than a day to do it means that you are not providing an up-to-date measure of how important each page is. Not up to date means not relevant and therefore not useful.

Brin and Page, together with Stanford computer science professor Terry Winograd, looked at the problem of ordering the Web through the prism of a network mapping problem and used yet another prism to look at that problem. They saw their problem was one of computational complexity—the complexity of processing the information furnished by the Web quickly enough to provide a useful measure of the importance of each page in a short amount of time. Existing procedures for calculating centrality measures for nodes in very large networks took too long, so they changed the frame of the problem from how to rank all of the pages of the World Wide Web in terms of relative importance to how to provide a good enough measure of the importance of each page in 24 hours, working with existing hardware and algorithms.

Their procedure, PageRank, disclosed in US Patent 6,295,999, calculates an approximate weight for each active web page based on the relative number of incoming ("cited by") and outgoing ("cites") links to neighboring pages. But it does not include all pages. Rather, it looks only in the local neighborhood of each page, circumscribed by a typical user's search radius—that is, her propensity to drop off, or randomly end, her search. It therefore includes a fudge factor that measures the probability the user will get bored and sign off or randomly surf to another page rather than to a page cited by the one she is currently looking at.

The resulting network is not nearly as dense as the real network of web pages, but it is good enough. Now the weight of each page—that is, its page rank, or Google centrality—can be calculated in only a billion billion billion operations. And what a difference a factor of a billion makes! The reduction in the time required to measure the relative importance of each page meant that existing hardware could be used to rank all 1 billion pages in less than 24 hours.

The information processing flexon sees various parts of a business as distributed problem-solving tasks. Information processing is computation that acts on unprocessed information (data) to produce processed information (predictions, root cause analyses, product designs, action plans). It can be concentrated in a single processor—a mind or a computer—or distributed among a number of different minds and computers, as is the case in a business. The flexon represents individuals, groups, organizations, firms, and markets as information processing units continuously engaged in solving problems and using different procedures—or algorithms.

When thinking, a mind uses its memory and perceptions—"inputs"—to solve problems by processing this information via a computational machine that applies an algorithm or a set of heuristics—a procedure—to the inputs to produce the outputs (behavior, or new thoughts). This procedure "runs" on the brain, which is the "hardware" in this picture: mindware is to brainware as software is to hardware.

The information processing flexon focuses our attention sharply on what information is used, how much memory and memory access cost, how costly each computation is, and how efficiently the computational device is at solving certain kinds of problems. It gives us a way of gauging the efficiency and effectiveness of a problem-solving process and the problem-solving prowess of a person, a group, or a business.

▶ YOU MIGHT WISH TO CONSIDER . . .

If all life is problem solving, then how would you model the problem you are solving while reading this very sentence by specifying
(1) current and desired conditions, (2) working memory requirements, and (3) the computational requirements for solving the
problem? What about the problem you are solving when you are
trying to balance a tray bearing five cups of hot tea with one hand?
What about the problem you are solving when applying the decision agent flexon to model lying or information distortion in an executive team?

THE EXPECTED VALUE OF COMPUTATION:
WHEN DOES IT PAY TO THINK?

Quite often the problems of business do not come in this form
(even though it is familiar from standard texts on managerial
decisions):

> Choose between a lottery with an expected discounted value of $100
> million and a lottery with an expected discounted value of $120 million.

Rather, they take this form:

> Choose between a lottery with an expected discounted value of $100
> million and a lottery that pays $600 million if the eighth digit place of
> the decimal expansion of the square root of 2 is a 5, and $0 otherwise.

Clearly computation can be very helpful, depending on how
costly it is and whether you know what you are doing. Suppose
you do not have a calculator. If you know Newton's method for
computing roots of natural numbers, based on the Taylor series
expansion of the function $f(x) = x^2 - 2$ around the value of
$f(x) = 0$, then you may be in business provided that you can implement the algorithm quickly enough to generate an answer in
the right amount of time The eighth digit is indeed 5: a gain of
$500 million for just seven steps of following a fail-safe procedure!
The juice *is* worth the squeeze, provided you have the right tool.

THE ART OF SIMPLIFICATION:
IT'S NOT WHAT YOU THINK BUT HOW

The information processing flexon helps us think about both whether to think and how to think about the business problem represented in figure 6.1: a sales representative who is trying to cover all of Canada's 4663 cities in the shortest amount of time. She has to be physically present in each city, and time (and gas) are expensive, so she wants to find the shortest path that connects all of these cities together. Looking at it through the information processing flexon lens, she begins by asking, "How hard is this problem?" It is a smart question in this case, because it is impossibly hard to solve by brute-force methods: she would have to consider some 4663 factorial permutations of cities making up the alternative paths, which would take current computational devices running at 10^{12} operations per second some 1.6×10^{1383} years to even enumerate. However, there is a method by which she can find the shortest path in just 6 minutes of (current) CPU time by using a solution search method put forth by Lin and Kernighan more than forty years ago.[1] Shown in figure 6.2, it involves guessing (of course!). The problem solver makes a guess at a plausible minimum path, makes small changes to it, evaluates the new path, retains it if it is shorter, and returns to the original if it is not.

This method is applicable to any problem that has the structure of the traveling salesman problem: computing optimal information and influence flows in a network of researchers (identify the minimal resistance path), optimizing the flow of materials and components on a production line (find the shortest path), optimizing the distribution system of a large logistics company (find the shortest travel time), and so forth.

Now suppose a hedge fund is asking for advice on a foreign currency speculation strategy that works as follows. For the 100 or so liquid currencies around the world, the strategy relies on exploiting

1. S. Lin and B. W. Kernighan, "An Effective Heuristic for the Traveling Salesman Problem," *Operations Research* 21 (1973):489–516.

Problem:
"Find minimum-length tour connecting
Canada's 4663 cities"

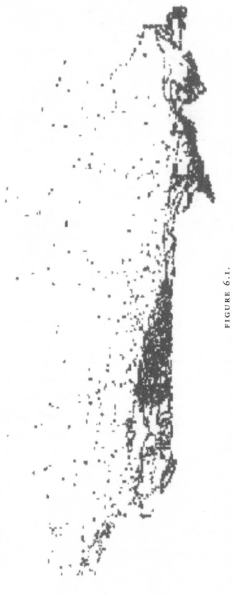

FIGURE 6.1.

Illustrating the traveling saleswoman problem. Source: Mihnea Moldoveanu, *Inside Man: The Discipline of Modeling Human Ways of Being* (Stanford, CA: Stanford University Press, 2011), 187. Used by permission.

Solution:

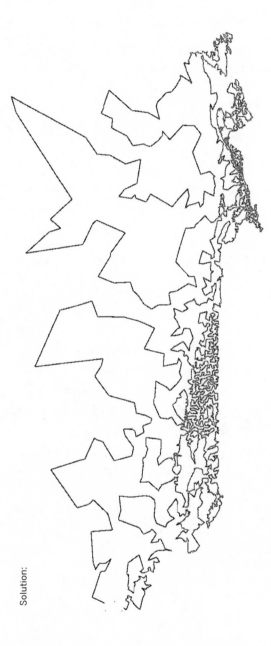

FIGURE 6.2.

The shortest path connecting Canada's 4663 cities, generated by the Lin-Kernighan algorithm. Source: Moldoveanu, *Inside Man*, 187. Used by permission.

the real-time difference in currency exchanges, net of transactions cost, and finding a conversion path from one currency to the same currency that makes even a very small—a fraction of a cent—profit over alternative closed paths. For instance, one can exchange US dollars into euros directly or, by changing dollars into yuan, yuan into yen, yen into shekels, shekels into rubles, and rubles into euros or going from dollars to yuan to rubles to euros directly. We represent the challenge as a path minimization problem similar to the traveling saleswoman problem: if there is a difference between the net cost of trading currencies along two or more different paths, then these differences can be exploited into a high-frequency trading strategy that makes net profits every few seconds—a sure way of turning the computational firepower you will need to calculate gains and losses along a large number of closed paths into profits.

Once you've shaped the problem in these terms, you can also figure out, for example:

- How powerful a computer you would need in order to solve the problem for any combination of currencies

- The combination of currencies most likely to produce arbitrage opportunities within a given period of time

- The paths connecting them most likely to produce supernormal trading profits

The information processing lens focuses on a core element of any business problem, namely, the number of operations required to solve it in the time we have. It drives us to ask, "How hard is it?" before attempting to solve the problem and to devise strategies for solving the problem more quickly and more accurately more of the time—for instance:

- How many combinations of N different features do we need to evaluate in building a new electronic vehicle for the mass market? Some 2^N of them, provided all combinations are feasible?

- How many different derivative securities can we put together if we start with n mortgages we can slice up in k different ways? Some *(nk)!* of them.

- How many different combinations of strategies are there in a market with M firms, each of which can play one of S different strategies? We may have to look at S^M of those—and that does not even include the analysis of each one of the combinations.

Doing a complexity analysis of the problem before trying to solve it can save staggering amounts of time and resources we would have spent simply tinkering with various candidate solutions (just imagine trying to solve the traveling sales representative's problem of Canadian cities by trial and error). We can figure out in advance which problems are likely to be intractable. We can then allocate time and effort to devising shortcuts to the solution when the problem has many variables and the required computational cost is likely to exceed the available time and resources.

The information processing flexon is the quintessential problem-solving language: it turns the elements of problem solving itself into the basic entities we use to model businesses. Simply put, through the lens of the flexon, businesses solve problems: their activities are problem-solving processes. We define a problem as a difference between where we are and where we want to be. To define a problem, we need to specify the set of current conditions—Where are we now?—and a set of desired conditions—Where do we want to be? We also need to specify a space of possible solutions—the combinations and permutations of the components of an admissible solution—for instance:

> *Problem*: Design a successful next-generation smart phone.
> *Solution search space*: A combination of all feasible modifications to the physical layer (hardware), network layer (communications), applications layer (operating system), and mechanical packaging.

Problem: Reduce the transportation and warehousing cost of a consumer good by 20 percent over two quarters.
Solution search space: All paths linking the manufacturing plant to the retail facilities and costs of each path.

Problem: Reduce political election forecasting error for the next congressional election by 20 percent.
Solution search space: All possible algorithms for processing available preelection data to improve forecast accuracy and reliability for the past 100 elections by 20 percent.

Solution search space in hand, we can focus on the specific way in which we search it: the algorithm. We can ask:

Is it deterministic, or does it involve guessing? We can understand the process by which a large multifunction bank (one that engages in retail, commercial, and investment work) searches for new opportunities for acquisition, for instance, using a guessing procedure that can be represented by a randomized algorithm. Since the number of possibilities is so large, the solution is to pick targets that have certain characteristics at random, evaluate their attractiveness, search for opportunities that most resemble these targets with respect to a certain feature (size), and evaluate them with respect to a performance measure (five-year profitability, say). This is then repeated until time runs out. The highest-performance candidate the search so far has produced is selected.

Is it serial or parallel? The problem of optimizing the distribution network of a large retailer can be tackled using a parallel search of all possible configurations of the distribution network, which may be a staggeringly large number, with sets of paths starting at different nodes assigned to different problem-solving agents, be they individuals or teams.

How long will it take someone using it to solve the problem in the worst-, best- and average-case scenarios? In other words, what is its time complexity? If we are trying to solve a dynamic pricing problem involving many buyers among whom we want to price-discriminate on the basis of the (sparse) information we have from their web footprint (e.g., search history), we need to figure out if the dynamic pricing algorithm can work quickly enough to calculate a price that is specific to each user in the time it takes the user to go from the product information web page to the product pricing page. Most problems are not solved by single agents—or single CPUs, for that matter. A configuration is an assignment of different problem-solving tasks to different problem-solving agents. Key variables are the specific problem-solving profile of each problem solver; for example, are they optimizers who consider all alternatives and pick the best one or satisficers who pick the first alternative that is better than a threshold? Can they optimize the process by which they optimize or tackle a problem only with known search methods)?

The problem-solving prowess of each individual agent is critical to determining the size of the problem a group of agents can solve, so we can ask: What is the hardest problem in terms of number of operations required for a solution in the worst- or average-case scenario that he or she can solve per unit of time?

The configurations of problem-solving agents are levers that we can access in redesigning the problem-solving process of a business: A risk management system may be best implemented as a parallel but synchronous process of evaluating covariances among different asset classes. But it is currently implemented in this business as a serial process that is overly burdened by the requirement for top-down decision making.

How do we measure the performance of problem-solving processes? Here is the easy case: the solution is quickly computed by a known method: you either get it or you do not. Here, the quality of the problem-solving process can be gauged by the speed with which the solution is synthesized from the problem statement and the available information. Management teams vary in the speed with which they make strategic decisions of the same quality, and this performance difference is often due to the procedures and algorithms that describe or prescribe the way they make decisions. For really hard problems, however—those that cannot be fully solved in the time available—we need a more sophisticated performance measure. It will take into account not only the speed of producing a solution, but also the accuracy of the solution and the reliability with which solutions of that accuracy can be produced. For instance, a network service provider making dynamic pricing decisions to maximize profit based on solving, in real time, a large-scale optimization problem may be able to produce solutions (bundles of features and associated prices) that are within 10 percent of the global optimum with 80 percent reliability (i.e., 80 percent of the time) given the time constraints (month to month) they face. Once we get to a figure of merit for the client's problem-solving process, we can seek to improve its prowess by changing the problem-solving procedures or algorithms it uses, changing the set of problem-solving agents, or changing the configuration of these problem-solving agents to increase any one or all of these characteristics of the problem-solving process:

- *Speed*: How quickly do you get to acceptable solution?

- *Accuracy*: How close to the optimal solution is it?

- *Reliability*: How predictably does the problem-solving process you use take you to an acceptable solution of the resulting solution?

CHALLENGE

A large telecommunications systems manufacturer, Company X, is facing a technological discontinuity in its core market. A new standard for the network layer of broadband wireless communication has emerged for both fixed and mobile applications. The standard has spawned a large number of start-ups, each of which has come up with a slightly different implementation of the standard, and led to several incompatible products. Telecommunications service providers—X's customers—are vying to be the first to market with the new class of hyperfast broadband connectivity, counting on the video games, online learning, and virtual reality markets to drive demand for bandwidth close to the 10X improvement offered by the new standard. Other telecommunications systems manufacturers—X's two or three competitors—have either started in-house development of their own products or made strategic investments in a few start-up companies funded by venture capital firms to develop products based on the new standard. The challenge for Company X is to come up with a viable solution to extend and consolidate its market leadership across the period of disruptive innovation that the novel technology will bring about in its industry, which is estimated to last between twelve and thirty months.

Using the information processing flexon, we focus on the technological disruption and the complexity of bringing a new product to market that is both compatible with most other products and delivers on the expectations of 10X bandwidth multiplication that telecommunications service providers are vying for. We specify the process by which a new network layer product is built as a three-step process: (1) design and implementation; (2) internal testing, interoperability, and external testing; and (3) network compatibility testing. We specify sufficient output measures for each process.

We estimate the time complexity of each of these processes by comparing the new network layer design with other network layers (3GPP, WiFi) that have been designed, implemented, tested, and deployed in the past in the same market, and defining classes of products that have similar measures of complexity to that of Company X's new network layer design. We estimate complexity by the (1) the computational complexity of the algorithms that must run in real time in order to implement the new protocol, (2) the worst-case complexity of an algorithm that tests for the compatibility of the new network protocol with other components of the network, and (2) the opinions of a panel of technical and market experts in the field. We may find that the new network layer is more complex than the WiFi layer but of similar complexity to the 3G network layer.

We use industry data to measure the time scales on which companies of different sizes, ranging from start-ups to the size of Company X, have solved problems of similar or greater complexity in the past on the basis of our estimates of the relative complexity of implementing, network-testing, and interoperability testing the new network protocol. We use company data to measure the speed with which Company X has solved problems of similar or greater complexity in the past.

We enumerate the feasible production and exchange arrangements by which X can bring a new product in this space to market. They will include straight-up acquisitions of one or more start-ups, followed by internal and compatibility testing using their technologies to arrive at a final product design; partnering with one or more start-ups by equity or convertible debt financing of their next rounds; strategic development arrangements, wherein X gets access or exclusive access to technology in return for a percentage of revenue or nonrecurrent engineering costs, a wait-and-see approach wherein X buys the winner of the technology arms race in this phase of the industry, without investing upfront; and fully internal development of a product based on the new standard. We use our measurement of the relative velocity of implementation and testing in different scenario for technological problems in the same complexity class to make predictions about the relative speed and quality of various feasible arrangements for delivering a compatible tested product within the next twelve to twenty-four months.

Now, for the optimization step: We evaluate the set of feasible arrangements with respect to the speed and quality of the solutions that are likely to be produced given the data we have. We may find, for instance, that (counterintuitively) buying many real strategic options by investing in many start-ups in the space is historically a poor strategy for problems of this complexity because of the internal competition for resources it causes at the level of X. Or we might find that developing the new product entirely from scratch internally is a poor strategy for products of this complexity because of the high coordination costs that arise within X-size firms and because of the super-incentive effects that an exit has for a small technology team—which exists in a small start-up but not within a technical team within X. We select and recommend the arrangement that is most likely to produce a viable, compatible product within the expected time frame.

TURNING THE LENS OF THE INFORMATION PROCESSING FLEXON ON OUR OWN PROBLEM-SOLVING PROCESS

The information processing flexon lives at a high enough level of abstraction that it can also be applied to the process by which we solve problems using any other flexon. Here, we are the problem-solving agents. We need to use the flexons to model the way we use flexons to model challenges as problems. Here is how:

- We encode the challenge in the language of the flexon.

- We articulate the problems of prediction and optimization that correspond to the challenge by specifying the variables we want to focus on and the relationships we think exist between them.

- We use the data we have to estimate and calibrate our model of the situation.

- We measure the currently unknown values of causally relevant variables.

- We drive to a desired solution, which is a well-defined problem statement on the first pass and one or more feasible solutions on the second pass.

Now we use the information processing flexon to carry out our optimization twice. First, we optimize the way we optimize. We identify the areas of our problem-solving process that are hard, such as enumerating the various combinations of firms and strategies in a large oligopoly once we have used the decision agent flexon to define a problem. We also optimize our search through feasible solutions by using maneuvers like randomization and parallelization to organize our search, or we configure the architecture of the problem-solving team to arrive at the optimal set of solutions in the minimum amount of time. Second, we use the search process we arrive at to find the search, optimally through the solution space.

▶ YOU MIGHT WISH TO CONSIDER . . .

How would you decompose the following optimization problems into double-loop optimization problems?

Design an application that maximizes your network footprint on the World Wide Web (be sure to define network footprint first)?

Dynamically adjust the price of your new Web 2.0 app in a way that best responds to the prices of all of your N competitors (take N to be at least 20)?

Design an information and data processing system that predicts the top line, bottom line, and year-over-year average revenue for a new pharmaceutical on a monthly, quarterly, and yearly basis?

FOR FUN AND PRACTICE: MORE CHALLENGES

Define and structure these challenges using the information processing flexon:

1. A quickly growing global online services provider found itself in a data capacity crunch much sooner than it had anticipated. The 88 megawatts of critical data on 100,000 servers around the world was forecast to double over the next three years. The tech team believed there had to be a better way to add capacity, especially given that internal analytics calculated average CPU utilization at less than 15 percent. The

company called for help to evaluate its infrastructure and data options and find a way to make future data growth more cost-effective.

2. This same global high-tech software provider asked for help in its development group to improve product development processes, which were characterized by long development cycles and inconsistent practices. Specifically, the firm needed help to induce the development team to realize the benefits of using appropriate and measurable metrics in software development and adopt lean and agile software development best practices that contribute to improving those benchmarks.

3. A major financial institution with significant holdings of collateralized debt obligations comprising concatenated tranches of mortgages from within very different risk default classes is seeking help with the identification of derivatives in terms of the risk associated with the probability of default of the mortgages they are based on.

Now define and structure each of these challenges using any one of the other flexons introduced earlier.

IF YOU WANT MORE: ANNOTATED REFERENCES

For an introductory text on computational complexity and tractability, see:

Garey, M. R., and D. S. Johnson (1983). *Computers and Intractability: An Introduction to the Theory of NP-Completeness.* New York: Freeman.

For an approach to representing human problem solving in terms of purposive symbolic manipulation, see:

Newell, A. C., and H. A. Simon. (1972). *Human Problem Solving.* Upper Saddle River, NJ: Prentice Hall.

For an introductory analysis of algorithms, see:

Cormen, T., C. Leiserson, and R. Rivest. (1991). *Introduction to Algorithms*. New York: McGraw-Hill.

For a primer on computational complexity and the measurement of the computational complexity of algorithms, see:

Papadimitriou, C. (1994). *Computational Complexity*. Reading, MA: Addison-Wesley.

For an application of the theory of computation and the use of computational processes to modeling phenomena in physics, biology, and perception, among others, see:

Wolfram, S. (2000). *A New Kind of Science*. Champaign, IL: Wolfram Research.

For an application of computational complexity theory to strategic games and strategic behavior, see:

Nisan, N., T. Roughgarden, E. Tardos, and V. V. Vazirani (eds.). *Algorithmic Game Theory*. Cambridge: Cambridge University Press.

For an application of information and computation theory to the modeling of mental behavior in human creatures, see:

Moldoveanu, M. C. (2011). *Inside Man: The Discipline of Modeling Human Ways of Being*. Stanford, CA: Stanford University Press.

7 PROBLEM SOLVING

AND THE DESIGN OF INSIGHT

We set out to design a platform that generates insight in a disciplined and reliable fashion. The eureka moment usually associated with insight is often viewed as a matter of luck—of fortuitous guessing after staring at a problem for a very long time.

Our thinking path suggests this picture is incorrect. Staring at business problems for a long time is nonsensical because there are no ready-made problems to stare at and because no business that has what it calls a problem will allow you the privilege of staring at it for a long time. There are no pre-defined problems, only predicaments, situations, and challenges. Turning them into problems requires an act of modeling. The critical moment for the generation of insight is the moment in which predicaments are turned into problem statements through models. Our flexons allow us to generate insight through depth, precision, and diversity of the models they let us build. Each flexon contributes a different way of seeing a challenge—letting us generate a different problem corresponding to it. Insight happens when we suddenly see something as something else, which allows us to make useful, unexpected associations and connections, and each flexon contributes a new set of something else in terms of which we can see the situation anew.

How we deploy the flexons makes a big difference to the quality and likelihood of the insight we can produce. We must resist the temptation to use them all at once without planning and sequencing our mental activity. Each flexon is a language in its own right. Its value is realized by using the expressive powers of its language fully to capture as much as possible of the challenge we are facing.

When we use the flexons conscientiously, at least two different problems framing strategies emerge: *redefine* and *refine*.

PATH ONE: REDEFINING THE CHALLENGE

We have built a technology for articulating different problems by shifting problem-solving languages and generating insights by focusing on different variables and relationships. When you face a challenge, choose a flexon, use the SEMPO (specify, estimate, measure, predict, and optimize) blueprint to define the problem in the language of the flexon, and generate a solution set. Then shift problems by replacing the flexon with another of the five flexons, and continue to repeat, as shown in figure 7.1.

The solutions generated by the use of the different flexons can be recombined to generate a broader solution set, based on having illuminated the challenge from radically different perspectives. As we showed in chapter 1, problem shifting can be understood as the kind of gestalt switching that goes on when you look at a graphical image designed to simultaneously represent two different objects, as shown in figure 7.2. Each interpretation of the figure focuses your attention on a different set of features. When you 'see' the word *liar*, you will notice the font, its style, imperfections, and ink blotches around the edges. When you see the profile of a human face, you may focus your attention on the shape of the nose, the expression on the face, or the direction of the gaze.

Equally important is what you are not seeing when you lock in on any one of these interpretations. You will not focus on the expression on the face or the direction of the gaze of the eyes when you see the word *liar*, and you will not focus on the font style and the quality of the calligraphy when you see the profile of the face.

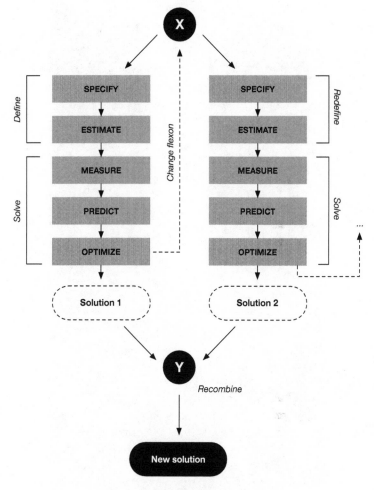

FIGURE 7.1.
Illustrating the shifting use of flexons to define and solve the same problem in at least two different ways.

FIGURE 7.2.

Bistable image that may represent either the word *liar*, written in calligraphic font (far left to low right) or the outline of the profile of the most striking features of a human face (seen from the right side). Source: http://www.sapdesignguild.org/goodies/optical_illusions/optical_illusions.pdf

Shifting problems by applying different flexons to the same challenge will allow you to bring certain variables into close focus while losing others. You will see more variables by increasing the number of ways in which you can see the challenge at hand in our example, which we shall call "herding cats," to significantly increase the productivity of the research and development effort of a large research-intensive biofuels manufacturer over five years.

The critical step of the SEMPO approach is specification: it maps observables into variables that we can estimate, measure, predict, and control. Let us walk through it with three flexons.

Networks Flexon

Specify the nodes (R&D workers), the links between them (three different networks, based on interaction, collaboration/co-inventorship, and interaction), and three different centrality measures for the nodes (degree, betweenness, eigenvector), representing informational advantage, knownness, and status. We can also define the augmented R&D network of the entire industry (nodes will be the researchers; ties will denote collaboration and co-citation). Measure three relevant centralities for individual researchers, and specify performance measures as normalized research output at the researcher and team level, which allows for the calculation of the effectiveness and efficiency of the system as a function of network structure. We can now estimate the relationship between node positions and productivity within the firm and the industry and predict the effects of redistributing ties throughout the system.

The challenge of designing a better innovation engine maps into the problem of designing a more efficient innovation network. We use the network flexon's variables to quantify and measure ours: Do the data confirm that information brokerage correlates with faster convergence to better ideas? We measure the rate of innovation in various parts of the network, whose topology we know. If the correlation is high, then design specialized reward systems for internal brokers—the high-betweenness centrality nodes. Does the problem require the coordination of many different fields of knowledge and expertise in different, disconnected parts of the network? If so, we create an internal knowledge market in which financial and status rewards accrue to researchers who communicate their ideas to co-researchers in a structured, auditable way. Does the firm's problem require the steady import of new ideas and techniques from other fields of knowledge? If so, encourage cross-pollination by setting up cross-discipline gatherings and information clearinghouses or wiki-style problem-solving sites that stimulate multidiscipline collaboration by using language systems accessible to multiple participants, trained in different fields.

What are we seeing? Through the prism of the networks flexon, we see ties and relationships, brokers and coordinators, cliques and subnetworks, and ways in which changing the topology of the network by altering the ways in which ties are formed can have an impact on performance.

What are we missing? We are not seeing process variables that describe the ways in which different ideas, modules, and techniques are put together. We are not seeing a full picture of incentives and decision rights. We are not seeing the complexity of the various research and development tasks and the relationship of this complexity to the overall task efficiency.

Now shift flexons.

Decision Agent Flexon

We specify the decision rights and incentives of each constituent of the research and development staff at the individual, group, and organizational levels. We map out the key incentives—financial and nonfinancial, including status and prestige—across teams and individuals. We specify an organizational performance measure for R&D productivity (patenting rate, expected commercialization value) and the individual payoffs (along the dimensions of individual incentives) resulting from given levels of organizational performance. We also specify the financial and nonfinancial benefits that accrue to individuals who initiate or terminate a search or continue a search that is already underway, and compare them with the net benefits to the organization of starting, stopping, or continuing to search along a given trajectory. We specify payoffs corresponding to search traps or failures as either type I (pursuing a development path unlikely to lead to a profitable solution) or type II (not pursuing a path likely to lead to a profitable solution) and use industry and company data to estimate the probabilities of these errors and their average costs for the business. We estimate relationships between decision rights allocation and incentives and overall performance at the industry level (best practices) to determine target performance improvements and predict ways in which we can bring them about by shifting incentives and decision rights. We can optimize the incentives of people involved in the research and development process to minimize type I errors (by incentivizing them to seek to reject apparent losers more quickly) or type II errors (by incentivizing them to persist along paths of uncertain payoff slightly longer than they normally would have). Within the modified incentive structure, we can allocate rights to initiate, implement, and ratify start-stop-continue decisions to individuals in the organization who represent the local maximum of two variables: the highest level of expertise and the incentives most closely aligned with the objective function of the organization.

What are we seeing? We now see decision rights allocations and incentives provisioned at the individual level as a function of organizational payoffs as key drivers of performance. We distinguish among various incentive structures that maximize R&D productivity.

What are we missing? We are missing the part of the picture that relates to the specific mechanisms by which different development paths and projects are generated and selected and the relationship between the quality and the cost of the generation process.

Now shift flexons again.

Now each R&D lab and the R&D process as a whole is seen as a population of ideas and techniques for producing new compounds and products. We can specify the rate and severity of the mutation or variation-inducing mechanism (new researchers? new techniques for synthesizing and refining compounds?) and the severity and rate of the selection process (Are ideas ranked relative to expected performance? Are they compared pairwise at the level of each lab? The firm as a whole? The industry as a whole? What happens to dominated ideas? Are they kept around? Are they rejected irreversibly? How frequently are new ideas filtered?). Answers to these questions will inform our study of best practices in terms of variation and selection mechanisms and rates across the industry and also across other industries (pharmaceuticals? alternative sources of energy?) aimed at estimating relationships between the characteristics of variation and selection processes and performance. We can also measure the specific parameters of the variation and selection processes used in the client's organization and make predictions about the effects of targeted changes in these processes to the performance of the overall process.

In the redefine mode, each flexon is used to formulate the challenge in a different way and generates insight by focusing attention on sets of variables and links among them that are not evident when the challenge is viewed through the lens of a different flexon. With each turn of the SEMPO crank, we see more: not only a bigger problem but also a different problem. Insight comes through the juxtaposition of radically different problem-solving languages in a new way: we see the interplay between incentives and selection mechanisms; between decision rights and the topology of the network; between the specific knowledge of the researchers and the rate at which new ideas are introduced as inputs to the R&D process; between the topology of the network—whether it has high or low degrees of closure—and the variation inherent in the candidate set of techniques. This is the essence of recombinant problem solving: radically different problem-solving languages generating insights in parallel when applied to the same challenge with a view to turning it into a precise problem statement.

PATH TWO: REFINING THE CHALLENGE

Some business challenges are so big that redefining the challenge into a separate problem while starting from scratch each time can turn into a massive process. Is there a way to deploy the flexons more efficiently? Indeed, there is. By hooking up the flexons in series and thereby concatenating them, as shown in figure 7.3, we can use each one to focus on the part of the situation or predicament that is left unaddressed or unsolved by the preceding flexons. For instance, the decision agent flexon gives us a good first-order model of the strategic predicament faced by a client who is competing in an oligopolistic market for telecommunication services. But it leaves us in the dark relative to the specific network and storage constraints that clients and service providers alike face. This is where the system dynamics flexon can step in to help by providing models of the flows of information among users that illuminate the bottlenecks and the most important areas for making strategic infrastructure investments. But the system dynamics flexon will not tell us all that much about the optimal topology of an access network, and that is where the networks flexon comes in handy. By modeling the effects on node-level satisfaction or performance of the topology of the access network as a whole, it allows us to see further and seek to optimize the way in which the client configures the network as a whole. And if we need to examine the interactions between the computational intensity of users'

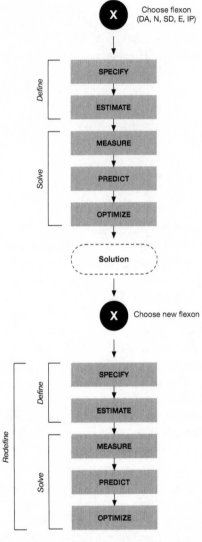

FIGURE 7.3.

Using flexons to refine problem statements. The flexons are used serially to focus on parts of the problem that emerge from the use of one flexon as black boxes in need of further analysis.

tasks and the utilization of the network as a whole in scenarios of massively distributed cloud processing of information and massive distributed gaming, then we can make use of the information processing flexon, which is tailor-made for just such a situation.

Consider this challenge, which we call "building a crystal ball." We focus on a multinational telecommunications service provider with significant investments in spectrum licenses around the world and several major broadband wireless fixed and mobile networks using a mix of 2.5G, 3G, 3.5G, and 4G technologies at the channel-coding layer, and a mix of circuit-switched and packet-switched technologies at the network layer. The CEO wants a five-year strategic outlook that takes into consideration shifting demographics, shifting technologies for connecting users with one another and with the core network (WiMax and LTE being the leading contenders for the riches of 4G), and shifting alliances and shifting groups of central players (Apple, Qualcomm, Google, Nokia-Siemens, Ericsson, Huawei, Alcatel-Lucent, ZTE, RIM). Where to start?

Decision Agent Flexon

Let's start looking at the situation through the decision agent flexon. Given that most service provider markets are oligopolies comprising two to five firms offering services to users on a fixed-price (to the user), extended-contract basis, thinking in terms of oligopolistic quantity and pricing games seems an intuitive place to begin. Users are agents that make buy decisions across service contracts on the basis of cost and features. The features are enabled by an infrastructure (access, equipment used to haul the cellular traffic back to the optical backbone, or backhaul equipment and spectrum) in which service providers have sunk significant costs or made irreversible investments, which determine the feasible quantity, quality, and pricing for the services offered (e.g., voice, video, data). Entrants are also agents that must incur significant sunk costs (licenses, equipment, marketing) to gain market share, calculating reasonable expenditure based on what they expect in terms of users and average revenue per user, figures that can be predicted by figuring out the oligopolistic equilibrium quantities given input costs and the elasticity of demand for service. The decision agent flexon allows us to calculate the equilibrium broadband cellular service prices and quantities in various oligopolistic markets, given our knowledge of the cost conditions that the different players face.

What about disruptive technological change? Enter 3.5G and 4G standards and equipment, along with new end-user equipment suppliers (Apple, Google), new end-user devices (smart phones, tablets), new operating systems supporting different applications (iOS, Android) and different levels of security (Data Encryption Standard, DES; Advanced Encryption Standard, AES), and physical and medium access control-layer technologies that differ with respect to spectral efficiency (bandwidth per user), coverage, and quality of service (Code Division Multiple Access, CDMA; Evolution-Data Optimized, Ev-DO; High Speed packet Access, HSPA; High Speed Uplink packet Access, HSUPA; Wireless Microwave Access, WiMAX; Long-Term Evolutionary, LTE). Enter also several new manufacturers of access equipment (Huawei, ZTE, HTC) that set new cost floors for the service provider's handset offering and cellular infrastructure capital expenditures. Thinking in terms of payoffs, strategies, and equilibria, we enumerate and evaluate the scenarios under which the client's competitors and potential entrants would use either existing technologies (GSM, including 2G, 2.5G and 3G, including EVDO and HSPA) or new ones (LTE and WiMax), and to work through one- to five-year scenarios under which new technology adoption in the industry either does or does not take place. The exercise sheds light on steady-state local market dynamics and the resulting free cash flows of the client under various assumptions about market penetration, revenue per user, and combinations of operating expenditures and capital expenditures.

Equipped with a picture of the industry that highlights the strategic options of the players, along with their cost structures and the expected payoffs of different combinations of strategies, we can predict the equilibrium outcomes (prices, quantities) in various geographic markets. Of course, the resulting combinations of strategies—and there will be 4096 of them with just four firms, each of which has six different strategic options at its disposal—will depend on assumptions about the infrastructure and technological core of the networks that will be deployed. These will typically be in the blind spot of a model of the industry generated by the decision agent flexon alone. To image that part of the challenge, we turn to the system dynamics flexon.

System Dynamics Flexon

To get better insight into how information in the form of error-free digital bits flows through the service provider network and what the main limitations imposed on the industry by infrastructure and technology are, we model the paths along which information flows from one user to another through a peripheral system—the access network—and a central system—the core network. We specify best-, worst-, and average-case user experience (probability of outage, bit error rate of received signal at different rates) as a performance measure for the system and can estimate the link between the efficiency of information flows through the network on the performance metric we have built.

We find that user experience is affected by the delays and degradations introduced by the buffers, wireless links, cellular base station protocols and processes, and backhaul links and their protocols, which can be estimated for various technologies that operate at the physical layer (CDMA, OFDM). The new picture allows us to make predictions about opportunities for strategic investments in infrastructure and technology that would significantly enhance the price-performance index of a network provider, and hence its competitive advantage, and opens up a search space for strategic complements and substitutes, such as public WiFi networks, that significantly enhance the trade-off frontier between coverage and capacity. We can distinguish more sharply between decisions to buy more spectrum and decisions to invest in using spectrum more efficiently by moving up on the telecommunications physical layer hierarchy ($2.5G \rightarrow 3G \rightarrow 3.5G \rightarrow 4G$). We have added texture to our analysis of strategic choices and their consequences by texturing the kinds of choices that a service provider can make. But it is not only the flow of information that is critical to these choices, but also the kinds of networks that these flows run on. So to focus on that part of the challenge, we use the networks flexon.

Networks Flexon

We ask about the different topologies of networks that a service provider can use to enhance the coverage-capacity frontier, subject to a constraint of cost to the user. The networks flexon allows us to pose and answer such questions expeditiously. It makes it possible for us to specify different dominant network topologies and thereby to distinguish between macrocell access networks wherein a single base station tower provides wireless service to thousands of users interspersed over hundreds of square miles and micro-, pico-, and femto-cell networks, wherein smaller and smaller base stations provide coverage for thousands, hundreds, or dozens of users and are themselves linked to central stations that aggregate their network traffic. Now we can make predictions regarding the capacity and coverage gains associated with each of these topologies. We take the networks flexon to another level of analysis and look to map the various social networks that are supported by wireless links (Which kinds of other users do most users talk to most of the time?) and adjust the topology of the overall access and backhaul networks to match that of the social networks of end users who want to connect to one another most readily and to adjust pricing plans according to these new models. Now we have even more texture around our problem definition: we see a new set of strategic choices related to the selection of optimal and adaptive network topologies. We may still feel in the dark regarding the evolution of the demand characteristics of the users, something that we can unpack only when we ask, "What do people use their smart phones for?" To image that, we use the information processing flexon.

Not all users of a broadband wireless network use the services of their provider just to communicate. The smart phone in its various guises has become a computational, text-editing, generalized problem-solving, game-playing device, and the range of services and solutions of a service provider can enable changes as well.

We want to specify and map out the technical innovations that will make a difference on a two- to five-year time horizon, and not just those that have enabled the current network infrastructure. The information processing flexon focuses us on the informational (memory) and computational (CPU power) resources required by end users to solve the problems that the smart phone has come to be used for. We map dominant applications—gaming apps, video streaming, Internet Protocol television (IPTV), word processing, online computing—in terms of the communication bandwidth that users need to successfully access them, the amount of memory they require at the level of the smart phone, and the amount of computational power they will need in their handheld device. We can then compare the requirements of these applications with the infrastructure capabilities currently in place in order to generate predictions about the technical solutions most likely to fuel the demand for new applications within five years.

We expand our overall user experience measure to include components related not only to the communicative use of the end-user device, the smart phone, but also of the computational uses of these devices. We can therefore expand the set of variables that describe the set of strategic choices of a network service provider by including hardware and software characteristics of the end-user device itself;. We can also estimate the impact of various levels of computational firepower and memory required by the user on the overall bandwidth and availability requirements of the network in different distributed intelligence scenarios (e.g., applications based on public, semiprivate, and private clouds and end-user device-based applications). Given a map of possible innovations, we can also ask about the likely hotspots for innovation activity, that is, the innovation hotbeds, and rate them according to their potential for introducing innovation, or unanticipated useful novelty, into the system. We may want to use the evolutionary flexon.

Evolutionary Flexon

The evolutionary flexon is a good flashlight for peeking into the unknown by illuminating the regions most likely to produce game changers. The broadband services industry represents the last stage in a linked chain of ecosystems of silicon, software, systems, and solutions providers that sell into the service provider (telecommunications) market, which sells into the end-user market. These industries can be specified as ecologies of firms, products, and solutions that vie with one another for survival ("fitness") in a competitive process that is more or less innovative ("mutation rate and temperature") and more or less selective ("single standard" or "open standard"; access to capital for weathering downturns and financing user equipment purchases; access to capital for financing geographical expansions, network topology modifications, technological shifts). Once we have specified the parameters of the evolutionary process that describes innovation at the level of silicon, software (applications, operating systems, network), systems (topologies, access protocols), and solutions (bundles of features and products), we can measure rates of innovation and variation and selection in the different segments of the industry and estimate the relationship between these variables and industry-shifting technological discontinuities across this and other industries.

Certain proxies for innovation may be useful indices to measures of evolutionary intensity. We measure the rate of patenting and new product introduction activity in various segments of the market as a proxy for the intensity of the competitive innovation landscape and the likelihood that the segment in question will generate alternative candidate technologies for the service providers. The market for smart phone applications can similarly be represented as an ecology of entities vying for promulgation, which can be modeled in terms of rates of variation and the properties of the selection mechanism: The rate at which iPad (as opposed to Android or Blackberry) applications are being developed and adopted can provide an index of both the survivability of the platform (think of it as the DNA of the system) and the probability that a solution to a significant system-level problem can emerge from that particular group of applications.

.   .   .

The flexon game is recursive: we can start all over again and turn the SEMPO cranks of different flexons for a second pass through the new, expanded problem statement we generated to go further in levels of specificity, accuracy, and coverage of our solution search space. The refine mode thus is an example of a recursively refinable process: each pass-through adds new insight.

KNOW·HOW, NOT JUST KNOW·WHAT

The use of flexons to define and structure business predicaments into solvable problems is not just a theory or a piece of know-what. Competence in the use of the flexons is not just knowing a bunch of terms and the rules by which these terms are put together to produce sentences. It is also know-how: a practice—the practice of business problem shaping. As with any other form of expertise, no amount of reading and memorization can replace practice as a path to mastery—some 10,000 hours of it, if we are to believe those, like K. Anders Ericsson, who have studied the learning curves of masters of their fields.[1] Because of the recursive and self-refining feature of the flexon methods, practice is not hard to come by.

Look at figure 7.4. It is a map of the challenges we have imaged in the languages of the different flexons in this book. It is meant to convey two things. First, the flexons taken as a whole form a comprehensive business problem solver's tool kit. We see challenges from operations, finance, strategy, marketing, human resources management, technology, and knowledge management and from industries ranging from consumer goods to health care, from pharmaceuticals to financial services, and from telecommunications services to biofuels engineering.

Second, there may be some initial preferential attachment of some flexons to some problems when we look at the map through an eagle's eye: of the decision agent flexon to challenges of performance management and top management team design; of the networks flexon to logistical and social media design challenges; of the system dynamics flexon to production and manufacturing challenges; of the evolutionary flexon to challenges of promotion, advancement, and selection; and of the information processing

1. K. A. Ericsson, R. R. Krampe, and C. Tesch-Roemer, "The Role of Deliberate Practice in the Acquisition of Expert Performance," *Psychological Review* 100 (1990): 363–406.

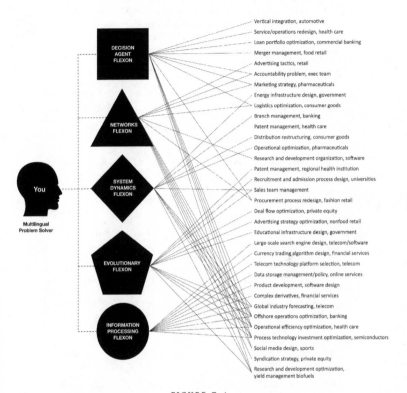

FIGURE 7.4.

The full suite of challenges we have tackled through the prism of the flexons. Note that each flexon can apply to several challenges to generate well-defined problems and produce insight through heightened precision and versatility.

flexon to challenges of task design and technology management. But we also see that each of these challenges can be illuminated to great advantage using one or more other flexons, which get you to see the challenge differently, so that when the marginal returns to thinking hard evaporate, you can generate brand-new insights by thinking differently.

Flexons are languages for representing ambiguous situations and predicaments as well-defined problems of prediction and optimization we can solve. They allow us to move up and down levels of analysis and delve into a problem to whatever depth is required to achieve more precision or more reliability in solutions. They also allow us to bring diversity inside the mind of the problem solver or problem-solving team, thus offering more opportunities to reach counterintuitive insights and innovative solutions. Instead of getting together a team of PhDs trained in the different formal languages each of the flexons represents, we can use the flexons directly to generate the knowledge map that the PhDs would have produced. The flexons are emulators for groups of heterogeneous problem solvers we have seen to be so productive at solving difficult problems. An executive or a consulting team that is adept at systematically using at least two or three flexons when addressing its trickiest problems will harness the power of this heterogeneity to expand its search space and stretch the realm of possible action—and maximize its opportunities for generating innovative and counterintuitive solutions to complex business problems.

THE PRACTICE OF FLEXONS

We are now routinely using the flexon approach in problem-solving sessions with teams of executives. The agendas of these one-day problem-solving sessions are organized around two or three flexons that we explore sequentially and in depth before a synthesis session at the end of the day. We also use flexons in parallel by having three teams of clients and consultants simultaneously consider the same problem, each team using a different flexon and providing as input to the joint synthesis session a one-page summary of the key insights generated by each flexon, which allows the team to quickly derive implications in terms of strategic initiatives or additional research to conduct.

Participants do not need more than a basic familiarity with the different flexons. We typically start by using flexons as problem-framing tools at the individual, group, company, or industry levels. They can be used initially to simplify situations by representing them in terms of a sparse set of variables then to increase the granularity of insight by unpacking the relationships between these variables, and by moving up or down levels of analysis. Insight deepens with the elaboration of each flexon and broadens with juxtaposition of solutions generated by different flexons.

The task left now is for you to apply the flexons to your own challenges, for it is only through practice that one gets to the level of problem-solving virtuosity that is worthy of the Carnegie Hall of insight. We have been relentlessly practice driven in the way we assembled our insight-generation vehicle, and it is in this spirit that we leave you with a few more challenges that should be approached using at least three flexons in both the redefine and refine modes.

FOR FUN AND PRACTICE: MORE CHALLENGES

Define and structure these challenges into solvable problem statements using the redefine and refine protocols for the use of flexons and at least three different flexons in each case.

1. A $100-billion asset base multipurpose North American bank is seeking help in redesigning its offshoring practices, ranging from call centers currently housed in India and Latin America to its technical risk management operations currently conducted in-house. A plan for an optimized vertical infrastructure for its operations over three to five years is sought.

2. The Ministry of Health and Long Term Care of a Canadian province that operates on a centralized health care provisioning model featuring a central insurer/payer (the government) that covers all health care expenditures of its population is seeking help in the implementation of fiscal, organizational, and developmental solutions that will reduce

its current $43 billion health care budget by 20 percent over ten years while improving health care outcome measures.

3. A $10 billion revenue multifabrication, multiproduct line semiconductor manufacturer with manufacturing operations in Europe, the United States, and the Far East is seeking guidance regarding its long-term (five years) investment plan in new products, new technologies, and new business development opportunities.

Made in the USA
San Bernardino, CA
15 January 2020